# Beethoven's Letters (1790–1826)

*From the Collection of Dr Ludwig Nohl*

VOLUME 1

EDITED AND TRANSLATED BY
GRACE JANE WALLACE

CAMBRIDGE
UNIVERSITY PRESS

# CAMBRIDGE
## UNIVERSITY PRESS

University Printing House, Cambridge, CB2 8BS, United Kingdom

Cambridge University Press is part of the University of Cambridge.

It furthers the University's mission by disseminating knowledge in the pursuit of
education, learning and research at the highest international levels of excellence.

www.cambridge.org
Information on this title: www.cambridge.org/9781108078481

This edition first published 1866
This digitally printed version 2014

ISBN 978-1-108-07848-1 Paperback

This book reproduces the text of the original edition. The content and language reflect
the beliefs, practices and terminology of their time, and have not been updated.

# CAMBRIDGE LIBRARY COLLECTION

*Books of enduring scholarly value*

## Music

The systematic academic study of music gave rise to works of description, analysis and criticism, by composers and performers, philosophers and anthropologists, historians and teachers, and by a new kind of scholar - the musicologist. This series makes available a range of significant works encompassing all aspects of the developing discipline.

## Beethoven's Letters (1790–1826)

Ludwig van Beethoven (1770–1827) was a prolific letter writer, with thousands of examples surviving to this day. Often written in great haste – 'in der Eile' was a common sign-off – they allow us to follow the great composer's anxieties and preoccupations, revealing the human figure behind some of the greatest music ever written. Despite the fact that 'many of Beethoven's letters slumber in foreign lands, especially in the unapproachable cabinets of curiosities belonging to various close-fisted English collectors', the German musicologist Ludwig Nohl (1831–85) published his collection of letters in 1865, and this two-volume English translation by Grace Jane Wallace (1804–78) appeared the following year, reflecting the fact that interest in Beethoven had not diminished nearly forty years after his death. Volume 1 includes the letter by the thirteen-year-old Beethoven which declares his life's commitment to the craft of music, and the still poignant 'Heiligenstadt Testament'.

Cambridge University Press has long been a pioneer in the reissuing of out-of-print titles from its own backlist, producing digital reprints of books that are still sought after by scholars and students but could not be reprinted economically using traditional technology. The Cambridge Library Collection extends this activity to a wider range of books which are still of importance to researchers and professionals, either for the source material they contain, or as landmarks in the history of their academic discipline.

Drawing from the world-renowned collections in the Cambridge University Library and other partner libraries, and guided by the advice of experts in each subject area, Cambridge University Press is using state-of-the-art scanning machines in its own Printing House to capture the content of each book selected for inclusion. The files are processed to give a consistently clear, crisp image, and the books finished to the high quality standard for which the Press is recognised around the world. The latest print-on-demand technology ensures that the books will remain available indefinitely, and that orders for single or multiple copies can quickly be supplied.

The Cambridge Library Collection brings back to life books of enduring scholarly value (including out-of-copyright works originally issued by other publishers) across a wide range of disciplines in the humanities and social sciences and in science and technology.

# BEETHOVEN'S LETTERS.

## VOL. I.

LONDON
PRINTED BY SPOTTISWOODE AND CO.
NEW-STREET SQUARE

BEETHOVEN.

Engraved by H.Adlard, from a Photograph of J.Mähler's Original Portrait.
in the possession of D.Th.G.v.Karajan.
Vice President of the Imperial Academy of Science, Vienna.

# BEETHOVEN'S LETTERS

(1790—1826)

FROM THE COLLECTION OF DR. LUDWIG NOHL.

ALSO HIS

LETTERS TO THE ARCHDUKE RUDOLPH,
CARDINAL-ARCHBISHOP OF OLMUTZ, K.W., FROM THE COLLECTION
OF DR. LUDWIG RITTER VON KÖCHEL.

TRANSLATED BY

LADY WALLACE.

*WITH A PORTRAIT AND FACSIMILE.*

IN TWO VOLUMES.

VOL. I.

LONDON:
LONGMANS, GREEN, AND CO.
1866.

# TRANSLATOR'S PREFACE.

SINCE undertaking the translation of Dr. Ludwig Nohl's valuable edition of ' Beethoven's Letters,' an additional collection has been published by Dr. Ludwig Ritter von Köchel, consisting of many interesting letters addressed by Beethoven to his illustrious pupil, H. R. H. the Archduke Rudolph, Cardinal-Archbishop of Olmütz. These I have inserted in chronological order, and marked with the letter K., in order to distinguish them from the correspondence edited by Dr. Nohl. I have only omitted a few brief notes, consisting merely of apologies for non-attendance on the Archduke.

The artistic value of these newly discovered treasures will no doubt be as highly appreciated in this country as in the great *maestro's* fatherland.

I must also express my gratitude to Dr. Th. G. v. Karajan, for permitting an engraving to be made expressly for this work, from an original Beethoven portrait in his possession, now for the first time given to the public. The grand and thoughtful countenance forms a fitting introduction to letters so truly depicting the brilliant, fitful genius of the sublime master, as well as the touching sadness and gloom pervading his life, which his devotion to Art alone brightened, through many bitter trials and harassing cares.

The love of Beethoven's music is now become so universal in England, that I make no doubt his letters will receive a hearty welcome from all those whose spirits have been elevated and soothed by the genius of this illustrious man.

GRACE WALLACE.

AINDERBY HALL:
*March* 28, 1866.

# PREFACE

## BY DR. LUDWIG NOHL

### TO THE

## LETTERS OF LUDWIG VAN BEETHOVEN.

In accompanying the present edition of the Letters of Ludwig van Beethoven with a few introductory remarks, I at once acknowledge that the compilation of these letters has cost me no slight sacrifices. I must also, however, mention that an unexpected Christmas donation, generously bestowed on me with a view to further my efforts to promote the science of music, enabled me to undertake one of the journeys necessary for my purpose, and also to complete the revision of the Letters and of the press, in the milder air and repose of a country residence, long since recommended to me for the restoration of my health, undermined by overwork.

That, in spite of every effort, I have not succeeded in

seeing the original of each letter, or even discovering
the place where it exists, may well be excused, taking
into consideration the slender capabilities of an individual, and the astonishing manner in which Beethoven's
letters are dispersed all over the world.  At the same
time, I must state that not only have the hitherto
inaccessible treasures of Anton Schindler's ' Beethoven's
Nachlass ' been placed at my disposal, but also other
letters from private sources, owing to various happy
chances, and the kindness and complaisance of collectors
of autographs.  I know better, however, than most
people—being in a position to do so—that in the
present work there can be no pretension to anything
approaching to a complete collection of Beethoven's
letters.  The master, so fond of writing, though he
often rather amusingly accuses himself of being a lazy
correspondent, may very probably have sent forth at
least double the amount of the letters here given, and
there is no doubt whatever that a much larger number
are still extant in the originals.  The only thing that
can be done at this moment, however, is to make the
attempt to bring to light, at all events, the letters that
could be discovered in Germany.  The mass of those
which I gradually accumulated, and now offer to the
public (with the exception of some insignificant notes),

appeared to me sufficiently numerous and important to interest the world, and also to form a substantial nucleus for any letters that may hereafter be discovered. On the other hand, as many of Beethoven's letters slumber in foreign lands, especially in the unapproachable cabinets of curiosities belonging to various close-fisted English collectors, an entire edition of the correspondence could only be effected by a most disproportionate outlay of time and expense.

When revising the text of the letters, it seemed to me needless perpetually to impair the pleasure of the reader by retaining the mistakes in orthography; but enough of the style of writing of that day is adhered to to prevent its peculiar charm being entirely destroyed. Distorted and incorrect as Beethoven's mode of expression sometimes is, I have not presumed to alter his grammar, or rather syntax, in the smallest degree; who would presume to do so with an individuality which, even amid startling clumsiness of style, displays those inherent intellectual powers that often did violence to language as well as to his fellow-men? Cyclopean masses of rock are here hurled with Cyclopean force; but hard and massive as they are, the man is not to be envied whose heart is not touched by these glowing fragments, flung apparently at random right and left, like meteors, by a mighty intellectual being, however perverse the treatment language may have received from him.

The great peculiarity, however, in this strange mode of expression is, that even such incongruous language faithfully reflects the mind of the man whose nature was of prophetic depth and heroic force ; and who that knows anything of the creative genius of a Beethoven can deny him these attributes ?

The antique dignity pervading the whole man, the ethical contemplation of life forming the basis of his nature, prevented even a momentary wish on my part to efface a single word of the oft recurring expressions so painfully harsh, bordering on the unæsthetic, and even on the repulsive, provoked by his wrath against the meanness of men.  In the last part of these genuine documents, we learn with a feeling of sadness, and with almost a tragic sensation, how low was the standard of moral worth, or rather how great was the positive unworthiness, of the intimate society surrounding the master, and with what difficulty he could maintain the purity of the nobler part of his being in such an atmosphere.  The manner, indeed, in which he strives to do so, fluctuating between explosions of harshness and

almost weak yieldingness, while striving to master the
base thoughts and conduct of these men, though never
entirely succeeding in doing so, is often more a diverting
than an offensive spectacle.  In my opinion, nevertheless, even this less pleasing aspect of the Letters ought
not to be in the slightest degree softened (which it has
hitherto been, owing to false views of propriety and
morality), for it is no moral deformity here displayed.
Indeed, even when the irritable master has recourse
to expressions repugnant to our sense of convention-
ality and which may well be called harsh and rough,
still the wrath that seizes on our hero is a just and
righteous wrath, and we disregard it, just as in
nature, whose grandeur constantly elevates us above
the inevitable stains of an earthly soil.  The coarse-
ness and ill-breeding, which would claim toleration
because this great man now and then showed such
feelings, must beware of doing so, being certain to
make shipwreck when coming in contact with the
massive rock of true morality on which, with all his
faults and deficiencies, Beethoven's being was surely
grounded.  Often, indeed, when absorbed in the unso-
phisticated and genuine utterances of this great man,
it seems as if these peculiarities and strange asperities
were the results of some mysterious law of nature, so

that we are inclined to adopt the paradox by which a
wit once described the singular groundwork of our
nature, ' The faults of man are the night in which he
rests from his virtues.'

Indeed, I think that the lofty morality of such natures
is not fully evident until we are obliged to confess with
regret, that even the great ones of the earth must pay
their tribute to humanity, and really do pay it (which
is the distinction between them and base and petty
characters), without being ever entirely hurled from
their pedestal of dignity and virtue.  The soul of that
man cannot fail to be elevated, who can seize the real
spirit of the scattered pages that a happy chance has
preserved for us.  If not fettered by petty feelings, he
will quickly surmount the casual obstacles and stum-
bling-blocks which the first perusal of these Letters may
seem to present, and quickly feel himself transported at
a single stride into a stream, where a strange roaring
and rushing is heard, but above which loftier tones
resound with magic and exciting power.  For a peculiar life breathes in these lines; an under-current runs
through their apparently unconnected import, uniting
them as with an electric chain, and with firmer links than
any mere coherence of subjects could have effected.  I
experienced this myself, to the most remarkable degree,

when I first made the attempt to arrange, in accordance
with their period and substance, the hundreds of individual pages bearing neither date nor address, and I was
soon convinced that a connecting text (such as Mozart's
Letters have, and ought to have) would be here entirely
superfluous, as even the best biographical commentary
would be very dry work, interrupting the electric
current of the whole, and thus destroying its peculiar
effect.

And now, what is this spirit which, for an intelligent
mind, binds together these scattered fragments into a
whole, and what is its actual power? I cannot tell;
but I feel to this day just as I felt to the innermost
depths of my heart in the days of my youth when I
first heard a Symphony of Beethoven's—that a spirit
breathes from it bearing us aloft with giant power out
of the oppressive atmosphere of sense, stirring to its
inmost recesses the heart of man, bringing him to the
full consciousness of his loftier being, and of the un-
dying within him. And even more distinctly than when
a new world was thus disclosed to his youthful feelings
is the *man* fully conscious that not only was this a new
world to him, but a new world of feeling in itself,
revealing to the spirit phases of its own, which, till
Beethoven appeared, had never before been fathomed.

Call it by what name you will, when one of the great
works of the sublime master is heard, whether indicative
of proud self-consciousness, freedom, spring, love, storm,
or battle, it grasps the soul with singular force, and
enlarges the labouring breast. Whether a man under-
stands music or not, everyone who has a heart beating
within his breast will feel with enchantment that here
is concentrated the utmost promised to us by the most
imaginative of our poets, in bright visions of happiness
and freedom. Even the only great hero of action,
who in those memorable days is worthy to stand beside
the great master of harmony, having diffused among
mankind new and priceless earthly treasures, sinks
in the scale when we compare these with the celestial treasures of a purified and deeper feeling, and a
more free, enlarged, and sublime view of the world,
struggling gradually and distinctly upwards out of
the mere frivolity of an art devoid of words to express
itself, and impressing its stamp on the spirit of the
age. They convey, too, the knowledge of this brightest
victory of genuine German intellect to those for whom
the sweet Muse of Music is as a book with seven
seals, and reveal, likewise, a more profound sense of
Beethoven's being to many who already, through the
sweet tones they have imbibed, enjoy some dawning

conviction of the master's grandeur, and who now more and more eagerly lend a listening ear to the intellectual clearly worded strains so skilfully interwoven, thus soon to arrive at the full and blissful comprehension of those grand outpourings of the spirit, and finally to add another bright delight to the enjoyment of those who already know and love Beethoven. All these may be regarded as the objects I had in view when I undertook to edit his Letters, which have also bestowed on myself the best recompense of my labours, in the humble conviction that by this means I may have vividly reawakened in the remembrance of many the mighty mission which our age is called on to perform for the development of our race, even in the realm of harmony—more especially in our Fatherland.

LUDWIG NOHL.

La Tour de Perlz—Lake of Geneva:
*March* 1865.

# CONTENTS

OF

# THE FIRST VOLUME.

## FIRST PART.

LIFE'S JOYS AND SORROWS.

1783—1815.

VOL. I.                                                   a

## SECOND PART.

### LIFE'S MISSION.

### 1815—1822.

## ILLUSTRATIONS.

# FIRST PART.

———•◇•———

## LIFE'S JOYS AND SORROWS.

### 1783 TO 1815.

# BEETHOVEN'S LETTERS.

—◆—

## PART I.

### 1.

*To the Elector of Cologne, Frederick Maximilian.*\*

Illustrious Prince,

Music from my fourth year has ever been my favourite pursuit. Thus early introduced to the sweet Muse, who attuned my soul to pure harmony, I loved her, and sometimes ventured to think that I was beloved by her in return. I have now attained my eleventh year, and my Muse often whispered to me in hours of inspiration : Try to write down the harmonies in your soul. Only eleven years old! thought I; does the character of an author befit me? and what would

---

\* The dedication affixed to this work, 'Three Sonatas for the Piano, dedicated to my illustrious master, Maximilian Friedrich, Archbishop and Elector of Cologne, by Ludwig van Beethoven in his eleventh year,' is probably not written by the boy himself, but is given here as an amusing contrast to his subsequent ideas with regard to the homage due to rank.

more mature artists say? I felt some trepidation; but my Muse willed it—so I obeyed, and wrote.

May I now, therefore, Illustrious Prince, presume to lay the first-fruits of my juvenile labours at the foot of your throne? and may I hope that you will condescend to cast an encouraging and kindly glance on them? You will; for Art and Science have ever found in you a judicious protector and a generous patron, and rising talent has always prospered under your fostering and fatherly care. Encouraged by this cheering conviction, I venture to approach you with these my youthful efforts. Accept them as the pure offering of childlike reverence, and graciously vouchsafe to regard with indulgence them and their youthful composer,

LUDWIG VAN BEETHOVEN.

2.

*To Dr. Schade,—Augsburg.*

Bonn, 1787. Autumn.

My most esteemed Friend,

I can easily imagine what you must think of me, and I cannot deny that you have too good grounds for an unfavourable opinion. I shall not, however, attempt to justify myself, until I have explained to you the reasons why my apologies should be accepted. I must tell you that from the time I left Augsburg* my cheer-

---

* On his return from Vienna, whither Max Franz had sent him for the further cultivation of his talents.

fulness, as well as my health, began to decline; the nearer I came to my native city, the more frequent were the letters from my father, urging me to travel with all possible speed, as my mother's health was in a most precarious condition. I therefore hurried forwards as fast as I could, although myself far from well. My longing once more to see my dying mother overcame every obstacle, and assisted me in surmounting the greatest difficulties. I found my mother indeed still alive, but in the most deplorable state; her disease was consumption, and about seven weeks ago, after much pain and suffering, she died [July 17]. She was indeed a kind, loving mother to me, and my best friend. Ah! who was happier than I, when I could still utter the sweet name of mother, and it was heard? But to whom can I now say it? Only to the silent form resembling her, evoked by the power of imagination. I have passed very few pleasant hours since my arrival here, having during the whole time been suffering from asthma, which may, I fear, eventually turn to consumption; to this is added melancholy—almost as great an evil as my malady itself. Imagine yourself in my place, and then I shall hope to receive your forgiveness for my long silence. You showed me extreme kindness and friendship by lending me three Carolins in Augsburg, but I must entreat your indulgence for a time. My journey cost me a great deal, and I have not the smallest hopes of earning anything here. Fate is not

propitious to me in Bonn.    Pardon my intruding on
you so long with my affairs, but all that I have said was
necessary for my own justification.

I do entreat you not to deprive me of your valuable
friendship; nothing do I wish so much as in any degree
to become worthy of your regard.  I am, with all esteem,
your obedient servant and friend,

L. v. BEETHOVEN,<br>Cologne Court Organist.

3.

*To the Elector Maximilian Francis.**

1793.

Most Illustrious and Gracious Prince,

Some years ago your Highness was pleased to
grant a pension to my father, the Court tenor Van
Beethoven, and further graciously to decree that 100
R. Thalers of his salary should be allotted to me, for the
purpose of maintaining, clothing, and educating my two
younger brothers, and also defraying the debts incurred
by our father.   It was my intention to present this decree to your Highness's treasurer, but my father earnestly
implored me to desist from doing so, that he might not
be thus publicly proclaimed incapable of himself sup-
porting his family, adding that he would engage to pay
me the 25 R. T. quarterly, which he punctually did.

* An electoral decree was issued in compliance with this request
on May 3, 1793.

After his death, however (in December last), wishing to reap the benefit of your Highness's gracious boon, by presenting the decree, I was startled to find that my father had destroyed it.

I therefore, with all dutiful respect, entreat your Highness to renew this decree, and to order the paymaster of your Highness's treasury to grant me the last quarter of this benevolent addition to my salary (due the beginning of February). I have the honour to remain,

Your Highness's most obedient and faithful servant,

LUD. V. BEETHOVEN,

Court Organist.

### 4.

*To Eleonore von Breuning,—Bonn.*

Vienna, Nov. 2, 1793.

My highly esteemed Eleonore, my dearest Friend,

A year of my stay in this capital has nearly elapsed before you receive a letter from me, and yet the most vivid remembrance of you is ever present with me. I have often conversed in thought with you and your dear family, though not always in the happy mood I could have wished, for that fatal misunderstanding still hovered before me, and my conduct at that time is now hateful in my sight. But so it was, and how much would I give to have the power wholly to obliterate from my life a mode of acting so degrading to myself, and so contrary to the usual tenour of my character!

Many circumstances, indeed, contributed to estrange us, and I suspect that those talebearers who repeated alternately to you and to me our mutual expressions were the chief obstacles to any good understanding between us. Each believed that what was said proceeded from deliberate conviction, whereas it arose only from anger, fanned by others; so we were both mistaken. Your good and noble disposition, my dear friend, is sufficient security that you have long since forgiven me. We are told that the best proof of sincere contrition is to acknowledge our faults; and this is what I wish to do. Let us now draw a veil over the whole affair, learning one lesson from it—that when friends are at variance, it is always better to employ no mediator, but to communicate directly with each other.

With this you will receive a dedication from me [the variations on ' Se vuol ballare ']. My sole wish is that the work were greater and more worthy of you. I was applied to here to publish this little work, and I take advantage of the opportunity, my beloved Eleonore, to give you a proof of my regard and friendship for yourself, and also a token of my enduring remembrance of your family. Pray then accept this trifle, and do not forget that it is offered by a devoted friend. Oh! if it only gives you pleasure, my wishes will be fulfilled. May it in some degree recall the time when

I passed so many happy hours in your house! Perhaps it may serve to remind you of me till I return, though this is indeed a distant prospect. Oh! how we shall then rejoice together, my dear Eleonore! You will, I trust, find your friend a happier man, all former forbidding, careworn furrows smoothed away by time and better fortune.

When you see B. Koch [subsequently Countess Belderbusch], pray say that it is unkind in her never once to have written to me. I wrote to her twice, and three times to Malchus [afterwards Westphalian Minister of Finance], but no answer. Tell her that if she does not choose to write herself, I beg that she will at least urge Malchus to do so. At the close of my letter I venture to make one more request—I am anxious to be so fortunate as again to possess an Angola waistcoat knitted by your own hand, my dear friend. Forgive my indiscreet request, it proceeds from my great love for all that comes from you ; and I may privately admit that a little vanity is connected with it, namely, that I may say I possess something from the best and most admired young lady in Bonn. I still have the one you were so good as to give me in Bonn, but change of fashion has made it look so antiquated, that I can only treasure it in my wardrobe as your gift, and thus still very dear to me. You would make me very happy by soon writing me a kind letter. If mine cause you any pleasure, I promise you to do as you wish, and write as often as it lies in my power; indeed everything is acceptable to me that can serve to show you how truly I am your admiring and sincere friend,

L. v. BEETHOVEN.

P.S. The variations are rather difficult to play, especially the shake in the *Coda*; but do not be alarmed at this, being so contrived that you only require to play the shake, and leave out the other notes, which also occur in the violin part. I never would have written it in this way, had I not occasionally observed that there was a certain individual in Vienna who, when I extemporised the previous evening, not unfrequently wrote down next day many of the peculiarities of my music, adopting them as his own [for instance, the Abbé Gelinek]. Concluding, therefore, that some of these things would soon appear, I resolved to anticipate this. Another reason also was to puzzle some of the pianoforte teachers here, many of whom are my mortal foes; so I wished to revenge myself on them in this way, knowing that they would occasionally be asked to play the variations, when these gentlemen would not appear to much advantage.

BEETHOVEN.

## 5.

### *To Eleonore von Breuning,—Bonn.*

The beautiful neckcloth, embroidered by your own hand, was the greatest possible surprise to me; yet, welcome as the gift was, it awakened within me feelings of sadness. Its effect was to recall former days, and to put me to shame by your noble conduct to me. I, indeed, little thought that you still considered me worthy of your remembrance.

Oh! if you could have witnessed my emotions yesterday when this incident occurred, you would not think that I exaggerate in saying that such a token of your recollection brought tears to my eyes, and made me feel very sad. Little as I may deserve favour in your eyes, believe me, my dear *friend*, (let me still call you so,) I have suffered, and still suffer severely from the privation of your friendship. Never can I forget you and your dear mother. You were so kind to me that your loss neither can nor will be easily replaced. I know what I have forfeited, and what you were to me, but in order to fill up this blank I must recur to scenes equally painful for you to hear and for me to detail.

As a slight requital of your kind *souvenir*, I take the liberty to send you some variations, and a Rondo with violin accompaniment. I have a great deal to do, or I would long since have transcribed the Sonata I promised you. It is as yet a mere sketch in manuscript, and to copy it would be a difficult task even for the clever and practised Paraquin [counter-bass in the Electoral orchestra]. You can have the Rondo copied, and return the score. What I now send is the only one of my works at all suitable for you; besides, as you are going to Kerpen [where an uncle of the family lived], I thought these trifles might cause you pleasure.

Farewell, my friend; for it is impossible for me to give you any other name. However indifferent I may be to you, believe me I shall ever continue to revere you and your mother as I have always done. If I can in any way contribute to the fulfilment of a wish of yours, do not fail to let me know, for I have no other means of testifying my gratitude for past friendship.

I wish you an agreeable journey, and that your dear mother may return entirely restored to health! Think sometimes of your affectionate friend,

BEETHOVEN.

6.

*To Herr Schenk.*

June 1794.

Dear Schenk,*

I did not know that I was to set off to-day to Eisenstadt. I should like to have talked to you again.

---

* Schenk, afterwards celebrated as the composer of the 'Dorf Barbier,' was for some time Beethoven's teacher in composition. This note

In the meantime rest assured of my gratitude for your obliging services. I shall endeavour, so far as it lies in my power, to requite them. I hope soon to see you, and once more to enjoy the pleasure of your society. Farewell, and do not entirely forget

Your Beethoven.

7.

*To Dr. Wegeler,—Vienna.**

. . . In what an odious light have you exhibited me to myself! Oh! I acknowledge it, I do not deserve your friendship. It was no intentional or deliberate malice that induced me to act towards you as I did—but inexcusable thoughtlessness alone.

I say no more. I am coming to throw myself into

appears to have been written in June 1794, and first printed in the 'Freischütz,' No. 183, about 1836, at the time of Schenk's death, when his connection with Beethoven was mentioned.

\* Dr. Wegeler, in answer to my request that he would send me the entire letter, replied that 'the passages omitted in the letter consisted chiefly in eulogiums of his father, and enthusiastic expressions of friendship, which did not seem to him to be of any value; but besides this, the same reasons that induced his father to give only a portion of the letter were imperative with him also.' I do not wish to contest the point with the possessor of the letter, still I may remark that all the utterances and letters of a great man belong to the world at large, and that in a case like the present, the conscientious biographer, who strives faithfully to portray such a man, is alone entitled to decide what portion of these communications is fitted for publication, and what is not. Any considerations of a personal character seem to me very trivial.

your arms, and to entreat you to restore me my lost friend; and you will give him back to me, to your penitent, loving, and ever grateful

BEETHOVEN.

8.

*To Dr. Wegeler,—Vienna.*

Vienna, May 1797.

God speed you, my dear friend! I owe you a letter which you shall shortly have, and my newest music besides. *I am going on well; indeed, I may say every day better.* Greet those to whom it will give pleasure from me. Farewell, and do not forget your

BEETHOVEN.

9.

*Written in the Album of Lenz von Breuning.*

Vienna, Oct. 1, 1797.

Truth for the wise,<br>Beauty for a feeling heart,<br>And both for each other.

My dear good Breuning,

Never can I forget the time I passed with you, not only in Bonn, but here. Continue your friendship towards me, for you shall always find me the same true friend,

L. V. BEETHOVEN.

## 10.

### *To Baron Zmeskall von Domanowecz.*

My cheapest (not dearest) Baron,

Desire the guitar-player to come to me to-day. Amenda (instead of an *amende* [fine], which he sometimes deserves for not observing his rests properly) must persuade this popular guitarist to visit me, and if possible to come at five o'clock this evening—if not then, at five or six o'clock to-morrow morning; but he must not waken me if I chance to be still asleep. *Adieu, mon ami à bon marché.* Perhaps we may meet at the 'Swan'?

---

\* As it appears from the following letters that Amenda was again at home in 1800, the date of this note is thus ascertained. It is undoubtedly addressed to Baron Zmeskall von Domanowecz, Royal Court Secretary, a good violoncello-player, and one of Beethoven's earliest friends in Vienna. The 'guitarist' was probably the celebrated Giuliani, who lived in Vienna.

### 11.

The musical Count is from this day forth *cashiered* with infamy.   The first violin [Schuppanzigh] ruthlessly transported to *Siberia.*   The Baron [see No. 10] for a whole month *strictly interdicted from asking questions*; no longer to be so hasty, and to devote himself exclusively to his *ipse miserum.**

B.

### 12.

#### *To Pastor Amenda,—Courland.*

Does Amenda think that I can ever forget him, because I do not write? in fact, never have written to him?—as if the memory of our friends could only thus be preserved !  The *best man I ever knew* has a thousand times recurred to my thoughts!  Two persons alone once possessed my whole love, one of whom still lives, and you are now the third.   How can my remembrance of you ever fade?   You will shortly receive a long letter about my present circumstances, and all that can

---

* Written in gigantic characters in pencil on a large sheet of paper. The 'musical Count' is probably Count Moritz Lichnowsky, brother of Prince Carl Lichnowsky, in whose house were held those musical performances in which Beethoven's works were first produced.  Even at that time he behaved in a very dictatorial manner to those gentlemen when his compositions were badly executed.  Thence the name given him by Haydn of ' The great Mogul.'

interest you. Farewell, beloved, good, and noble friend! Ever continue your love and friendship towards me, just as I shall ever be your faithful

BEETHOVEN.

## 13.

### *To Pastor Amenda.*

1800.

My dear, my good Amenda, my warm-hearted Friend, I received and read your last letter with deep emotion, and with mingled pain and pleasure. To what can I compare your fidelity and devotion to me! Ah! it is indeed delightful that you still continue to love me so well. I know how to prize you, and to distinguish you from all others; you are not like my Vienna friends. No! you are one of those whom the soil of my fatherland is wont to bring forth: how often I wish that you were with me, for your Beethoven is very unhappy. You must know that one of my most precious faculties, that of hearing, is become very defective; even while you were still with me I felt indications of this, though I said nothing, but it is now much worse. Whether I shall ever be cured remains yet to be seen: it is supposed to proceed from the state of my digestive organs, but I am almost entirely recovered in that respect. I hope indeed that my hearing may improve, but I scarcely think so, for attacks of this kind are the most incurable of all. How sad my life must now be!—forced to shun all that is most dear and precious to me, and to live with such miserable egotists as ——— &c. I can with truth say that of all my friends Lichnowsky [Prince Carl] is the most genuine. He last year settled 600 florins on me, which, together with the good sale of my works, enables me to live free from care as to my maintenance. All that I now write I can dispose of five times over, and be well paid into the bargain. I have been writing a good deal latterly, and as I hear that you have ordered some pianos from ———, I will send you some of my compositions in the packing-case of one of these instruments, by which means they will not cost you so much.

To my great comfort, a person has returned here with whom I can enjoy the pleasures of society and disinterested friendship,—one of the friends of my youth [Stephan von Breuning]. I have often spoken to him of you, and told him that since I left my fatherland, you are one of those to whom my heart specially clings. Z. [Zmeskall?] does not seem quite to please him; he is, and always will be, too weak for true friendship, and I look on him and ——— as mere instruments on which I play as I please, but never can they bear noble testimony to my inner and outward energies, or feel true sympathy with me: I value them only in so far as their services deserve. Oh! how happy should I now be, had I my full sense of hearing; I would then hasten to you, whereas as it is, I must withdraw from every-

thing. My best years will thus pass away, without
effecting what my talents and powers might have enabled me to perform. How melancholy is the resignation in which I must take refuge! I had determined
to rise superior to all this, but how is it possible?
If in the course of six months my malady be pronounced incurable, then, Amenda! I shall appeal to
you to leave all else and come to me, when I intend to
travel (my affliction is less distressing when playing
and composing, and most so in intercourse with others),
and you must be my companion. I have a conviction
that good fortune will not forsake me, for to what may
I not at present aspire? Since you were here I have
written everything except Operas and church music.
You will not, I know, refuse my petition; you will
help your friend to bear his burden and his calamity.
I have also very much perfected my pianoforte playing,
and I hope that a journey of this kind may possibly
contribute to your own success in life, and you would
thenceforth always remain with me. I duly received
all your letters, and though I did not reply to them, you
were constantly present with me, and my heart beats
as tenderly as ever for you. I beg you will keep the
fact of my deafness a profound secret, and not confide it
to any human being. Write to me frequently: your
letters, however short, console and cheer me, so I shall
soon hope to hear from you.

Do not give your Quartett to anyone [in F, Op. 18,

No. 1], as I have altered it very much, having only now
succeeded in writing Quartetts properly: this you will
at once perceive when you receive it. Now, farewell, my
dear kind friend! If by any chance I can serve you
here, I need not say that you have only to command me.

Your faithful and truly attached

L. v. BEETHOVEN.

### 14.

#### To Wegeler.

Vienna, June 29, 1800.

My dear and valued Wegeler,

How much I thank you for your remembrance of
me, little as I deserve it, or have sought to deserve it;
and yet you are so kind that you allow nothing, not
even my unpardonable neglect, to discourage you, always remaining the same true, good, and faithful friend.
That I can ever forget you or yours, once so dear and
precious to me, do not for a moment believe. There
are times when I find myself longing to see you again,
and wishing that I could go to stay with you. My
fatherland, that lovely region where I first saw the light,
is still as distinct and beauteous in my eyes as when
I quitted you; in short, I shall esteem the time when
I once more see you, and again greet Father Rhine, as
one of the happiest periods of my life. When this may
be I cannot yet tell, but at all events I may say that
you shall not see me again till I have become eminent,

not only as an artist, but better and more perfect as a man; and if the condition of our fatherland be then more prosperous, my art shall be entirely devoted to the benefit of the poor. Oh, blissful moment!—how happy do I esteem myself that I can expedite it and bring it to pass!

You desire to know something of my position: well! it is by no means bad. However incredible it may appear, I must tell you that Lichnowsky has been, and still is, my warmest friend (slight dissensions occurred occasionally between us, and yet they only served to strengthen our friendship). He settled on me last year the sum of 600 florins, for which I am to draw on him till I can procure some suitable situation. My compositions are very profitable, and I may really say that I have almost more commissions than it is possible for me to execute: I can have six or seven publishers or more for every piece if I choose: they no longer bargain with me—I demand, and they pay—so you see this is a very good thing. For instance, I have a friend in distress, and my purse does not admit of my assisting him at once, but I have only to sit down and write, and in a short time he is relieved. I am also become more economical than formerly. If I finally settle here, I don't doubt I shall be able to secure a particular day every year for a concert, of which I have already given several. That malicious demon, however, bad health, has been a stumblingblock in my path  my hearing during the last three years has become gradually worse. The chief cause of this infirmity proceeds from the state of my digestive organs, which, as you know, were formerly bad enough, but have latterly become much worse, and being constantly afflicted with diarrhœa, has brought on extreme weakness. Frank [Director of the General Hospital] strove to restore the tone of my digestion by tonics, and my hearing by oil of almonds; but alas! these did me no good whatever; my hearing became worse, and my digestion continued in its former plight. This went on till the autumn of last year, when I was often reduced to utter despair. Then some medical *asinus* recommended me cold baths, but a more judicious doctor the tepid ones of the Danube, which did wonders for me; my digestion improved, but my hearing remained the same, or in fact rather got worse. I did indeed pass a miserable winter; I suffered from most dreadful spasms, and sank back into my former condition. Thus it went on till about a month ago, when I consulted Vering [an army surgeon], under the belief that my maladies required surgical advice; besides, I had every confidence in him. He succeeded in almost entirely checking the violent diarrhœa, and ordered me the tepid baths of the Danube, into which I pour some strengthening mixture. He gave me no medicine, except some digestive pills four days ago, and a lotion for my ears. I certainly do feel better and stronger, but my ears are buzzing and ringing perpetually, day and night

I can with truth say that my life is very wretched; for nearly two years past I have avoided all society, because I find it impossible to say to people, *I am deaf!* In any other profession this might be more tolerable, but in mine such a condition is truly frightful. Besides, what would my enemies say to this?—and they are not few in number.

To give you some idea of my extraordinary deafness, I must tell you that in the theatre I am obliged to lean close up against the orchestra in order to understand the actors, and when a little way off I hear none of the high notes of instruments or singers. It is most astonishing that in conversation some people never seem to observe this; being subject to fits of absence, they attribute it to that cause. I often can scarcely hear a person if speaking low; I can distinguish the tones but not the words, and yet I feel it intolerable if anyone shouts to me. Heaven alone knows how it is to end! Vering declares that I shall certainly improve, even if I be not entirely restored. How often have I cursed my existence! Plutarch led me to resignation. I shall strive if possible to set Fate at defiance, although there must be moments in my life when I cannot fail to be the most unhappy of God's creatures. I entreat you to say nothing of my affliction to anyone, not even to Lorchen [see Nos. 4 and 5]. I confide the secret to you alone, and entreat you some day to correspond with Vering on the subject. If I continue in the same state,

I shall come to you in the ensuing spring, when you must engage a house for me somewhere in the country, amid beautiful scenery, and I shall then become a rustic for a year, which may perhaps effect a change.  Resignation !—what a miserable refuge! and yet it is my sole remaining one.  You will forgive my thus appealing to your kindly sympathies at a time when your own position is sad enough.  Stephan Breuning is here, and we are together almost every day: it does me so much good to revive old feelings !  He has really become a capital good fellow, not devoid of talent, and his heart, like that of us all, pretty much in the right place. [See No. 13.]

I have very charming rooms at present adjoining the Bastei [the ramparts], and peculiarly valuable to me on account of my health [at Baron Pasqualati's].  I do really think I shall be able to arrange that Breuning shall come to me.  You shall have your Antiochus [a picture], and plenty of my music besides—if, indeed, it will not cost you too much.  Your love of art does honestly rejoice me.  Only say how it is to be done, and I will send you all my works, which now amount to a considerable number, and are daily increasing.  I beg you will let me have my grandfather's portrait as soon as possible by the post, in return for which I send you that of his grandson, your loving and attached Beethoven.  It has been brought out here by Artaria, who, as well as many other publishers, has often urged this on me. I intend soon to write to Stoffeln [Christoph von Breuning], and plainly admonish him about his surly humour. I mean to sound in his ears our old friendship, and to insist on his promising me not to annoy you further in your sad circumstances. I will also write to the amiable Lorchen. Never have I forgotten one of you, my kind friends, though you did not hear from me; but you know well that writing never was my *forte*, even my best friends having received no letters from me for years. I live wholly in my music, and scarcely is one work finished when another is begun; indeed I am now often at work on three or four things at the same time. Do write to me frequently, and I will strive to find time to write to you also. Give my remembrances to all, especially to the kind Frau Hofräthin [von Breuning], and say to her that I am still subject to an occasional *raptus*. As for K——, I am not at all surprised at the change in her; Fortune rolls like a ball, and does not always stop before the best and noblest. As to Ries [Court musician in Bonn], to whom pray cordially remember me, I must say one word. I will write to you more particularly about his son [Ferdinand], although I believe that he would be more likely to succeed in Paris than in Vienna, which is already overstocked, and where even those of the highest merit find it a hard matter to maintain themselves. By next autumn or winter, I shall be able to see what can be done for him, because then all the world returns to town.  Farewell, my kind, faithful Wegeler!  Rest assured of the love and friendship of your

BEETHOVEN.

15.

To Countess Giulietta Guicciardi.*

Morning, July 6, 1800.

My angel! my all! my second self!

Only a few words to-day, written with a pencil (your own).  My residence cannot be settled till to-morrow.  What a tiresome loss of time!  Why this deep grief when necessity compels?—can our love exist without sacrifices, and by refraining from desiring all things?  Can you alter the fact that you are not wholly mine, nor I wholly yours?  Ah! contemplate the beauties of nature, and reconcile your spirit to the inevitable.  Love demands all, and has a right to do so, and thus it is *I feel towards you,* and *you towards me*; but you do not

---

* These letters to his 'immortal beloved' to whom the C sharp minor Sonata is dedicated, appear here for the first time in their integrity, in accordance with the originals written in pencil on fine note-paper, and given in Schindler's 'Beethoven's Nachlass.'  There has been much discussion about the date.  It is certified, in the first place, in the church register which Alex. Thayer saw in Vienna, that Giulietta was married to Count Gallenberg in 1801; and in the next place, the 6th of July falls on a Monday in 1800.  The other reasons which induce me decidedly to fix this latter year as the date of the letter, I mean to give at full length in the second volume of 'Beethoven's Biography.'  I may also state that Beethoven was at baths in Hungary at that time.  Whether the K—— in the second letter means Komorn, I cannot tell.

sufficiently remember that I must live both *for you* and
*for myself.* Were we wholly united, you would feel this
sorrow as little as I should. My journey was terrible.
I did not arrive here till four o'clock yesterday morning,
as no horses were to be had. The drivers chose another
route; but what a dreadful one it was! At the last
stage I was warned not to travel through the night, and
to beware of a certain wood, but this only incited me to
go forward, and I was wrong. The carriage broke down,
owing to the execrable roads, mere deep rough country
lanes, and had it not been for the postilions I must have
been left by the wayside. Esterhazy, travelling the usual
road, had the same fate with eight horses, whereas I had
only four. Still I felt a certain degree of pleasure, which
I invariably do when I have happily surmounted any
difficulty. But I must now pass from the outer to the
inner man. We shall, I trust, soon meet again; to-day
I cannot impart to you all the reflections I have made,
during the last few days, on my life; were our hearts
closely united for ever, none of these would occur to
me. My heart is overflowing with all I have to say to
you. Ah! there are moments when I find that speech is
actually nothing. Take courage! Continue to be ever
my true and only love, my all! as I am yours. The gods
must ordain what is further to be and shall be!

Your faithful<br>LUDWIG.

Monday evening, July 6.

You grieve! dearest of all beings! I have just heard that the letters must be sent off very early. Mondays and Thursdays are the only days when the post goes to K. from here. You grieve! Ah! where I am, there you are ever with me: how earnestly shall I strive to pass my life with you, and what a life will it be!!! Whereas now!! without you!! and persecuted by the kindness of others, which I neither deserve nor try to deserve! The servility of man towards his fellow-man pains me, and when I regard myself as a component part of the universe, what am I, what is he who is called the greatest?—and yet herein are displayed the godlike feelings of humanity!—I weep in thinking that you will receive no intelligence from me till probably Saturday. However dearly you may love me, I love you more fondly still. Never conceal your feelings from me. Good night! As a patient at these baths, I must now go to rest [a few words are here effaced by Beethoven himself]. Oh, heavens! so near, and yet so far! Is not our love a truly celestial mansion, but firm as the vault of heaven itself?

July 7.

Good morning!

Even before I rise, my thoughts throng to you, my immortal beloved!—sometimes full of joy, and yet again sad, waiting to see whether Fate will hear us. I must live either wholly with you, or not at all. Indeed I have resolved to wander far from you [see No. 13] till the moment arrives when I can fly into your arms, and feel that they are my home, and send forth my soul in unison with yours into the realm of spirits. Alas! it must be so! You will take courage, for you know my fidelity. Never can another possess my heart—never, never! Oh, heavens! Why must I fly from her I so fondly love? and yet my existence in W. was as miserable as here. Your love made me the most happy and yet the most unhappy of men. At my age, life requires a uniform equality; can this be found in our mutual relations? My angel! I have this moment heard that the post goes every day, so I must conclude, that you may get this letter the sooner. Be calm! for we can only attain our object of living together by the calm contemplation of our existence. Continue to love me. Yesterday, to-day, what longings for you, what tears for you! for you! for you! my life! my all! Farewell! Oh! love me for ever, and never doubt the faithful heart of your lover,

L.

Ever thine.
Ever mine.
Ever each other's.

16.

*To Matthisson.*

Vienna, August 4, 1800.

Most esteemed Friend,

You will receive with this one of my compositions published some years since, and yet, to my shame, you probably have never heard of it. I cannot attempt to excuse myself, or to explain why I dedicated a work to you which came direct from my heart, but never acquainted you with its existence, unless indeed in this way, that at first I did not know where you lived, and partly also from diffidence, which led me to think I might have been premature in dedicating a work to you before ascertaining that you approved of it. Indeed even now I send you ' Adelaide' with a feeling of timidity. You know yourself what changes the lapse of some years brings forth in an artist who continues to make progress ; the greater the advances we make in art, the less are we satisfied with our works of an earlier date. My most ardent wish will be fulfilled if you are not dissatisfied with the manner in which I have set your heavenly ' Adelaide' to music, and are incited by it soon to compose a similar poem ; and if you do not consider my request too indiscreet, I would ask you to send it to me forthwith, that I may exert all my energies to approach your lovely poetry in merit. Pray regard the dedication as a token of the pleasure which your

' Adelaide' conferred on me, as well as of the appreciation and intense delight your poetry always has inspired,
and *always will inspire in me.*

When playing ' Adelaide,' sometimes recall

Your sincere admirer,

BEETHOVEN.

17.

*To Frau Frank,—Vienna.*

October 1800.

Dear Lady,

At the second announcement of our concert, you
must remind your husband that the public should
be made acquainted with the names of those whose
talents are to contribute to this concert. Such is
the custom here; and indeed, were it not so, what is
there to attract a larger audience? which is after all
our chief object. Punto [the celebrated horn-player, for
whom Beethoven wrote Sonata 17] is not a little indignant about the omission, and I must say he has reason
to be so, but even before seeing him it was my intention
to have reminded you of this, for I can only explain the
mistake by great haste or great forgetfulness. Be so
good, then, dear lady, as to attend to my hint, otherwise
you will certainly expose yourself to *many annoyances.*
Being at last convinced in my own mind, and by others,
that I shall not be quite superfluous in this concert, I
know that not only I, but also Punto, Simoni [a tenor-
ist], and Galvani will demand that the public should be

apprised of our zeal for this charitable object, otherwise
we must all conclude that we are not wanted.

Yours,

BEETHOVEN.

18.

*To Herr von Wegeler.*

Vienna, Nov. 16, 1800.

My dear Wegeler,

I thank you for this fresh proof of your interest in
me, especially as I so little deserve it. You wish to
know how I am, and what remedies I use. Unwilling
as I always feel to discuss this subject, still I feel less
reluctant to do so with you than with any other person.
For some months past, Vering has ordered me to apply
blisters on both arms of a particular kind of bark, with
which you are probably acquainted; a disagreeable
remedy, independent of the pain, as it deprives me of
the free use of my arms for a couple of days at a time,
till the blisters have drawn sufficiently. The ringing
and buzzing in my ears have certainly rather de-
creased, particularly in the left ear, in which the
malady first commenced, but my hearing is not at
all improved; in fact I fear that it is become rather
worse. My health is better, and after using the tepid
baths for a time, I feel pretty well for eight or ten days.
I seldom take tonics, but I have begun applications of
herbs, according to your advice. Vering will not hear

of plunge baths, but I am much dissatisfied with him; he is neither so attentive nor so indulgent as he ought to be to such a malady: if I did not go to him, which is no easy matter, I should never see him at all. What is your opinion of Schmidt [an army surgeon]? I am unwilling to make any change, but it seems to me that Vering is too much of a practitioner to acquire new ideas by reading. On this point Schmidt appears to be a very different man, and would probably be less negligent with regard to my case. I hear wonders of galvanism; what do you say to it? A physician told me that he knew a deaf and dumb child whose hearing was restored by it (in Berlin), and likewise a man who had been deaf for seven years, and recovered his hearing. I am told that your friend Schmidt is at this moment making experiments on the subject.

I am now leading a somewhat more agreeable life, as of late I have been associating more with other people. You could scarcely believe what a sad and dreary life mine has been for the last two years; my defective hearing everywhere pursuing me like a spectre, making me fly from every one, and appear a misanthrope; and yet no one is in reality less so! This change has been wrought by a lovely fascinating girl [undoubtedly Giulietta], who loves me, and whom I love. I have once more had some blissful moments during the last two years, and it is the first time I ever felt that marriage could make me happy. Unluckily, she is not in my rank of life, and indeed at this moment I can marry no one; I must first bestir myself actively in the world.   Had it not been for my deafness, I would have travelled half round the globe ere now, and this I must still do.   For me there is no pleasure so great as to promote and to pursue my art.

Do not suppose that I could be happy with you. What indeed could make me happier?  Your very solicitude would distress me; I should read your compassion every moment in your countenance, which would make me only still more unhappy.  What were my thoughts amid the glorious scenery of my fatherland? The hope alone of a happier future, which would have been mine but for this affliction!  Oh! I could span the world were I only free from this!  I feel that my youth is only now commencing.  Have I not always been an infirm creature?  For some time past my bodily strength has been increasing, and it is the same with my mental powers.   I feel, though I cannot describe it, that I daily approach the object I have in view, in which alone can your Beethoven live.  No rest for him! —I know of none but in sleep, and I do grudge being obliged to sacrifice more time to it than formerly.*   Were I only half cured of my malady, then I would come to you, and, as a more perfect and mature man, renew our old friendship.

* 'Too much sleep is hurtful' is marked by a thick score in the Odyssey (45, 393) by Beethoven's hand.  See Schindler's 'Beethoven's Nachlass.'

You should then see me as happy as I am ever destined to be here below—not unhappy. No! that I could not endure; I will boldly meet my fate, never shall it succeed in crushing me. Oh! it is so glorious to live one's life a thousand times over! I feel that I am no longer made for a quiet existence. You will write to me as soon as possible? Pray try to prevail on Steffen [von Breuning] to seek an appointment from the Teutonic Order somewhere. Life here is too harassing for his health; besides, he is so isolated that I do not see how he is ever to get on. You know the kind of existence here. I do not take it upon myself to say that society would dispel his lassitude, but he cannot be persuaded to go anywhere. A short time since, I had some music in my house, but our friend Steffen stayed away. Do recommend him to be more calm and self-possessed, which I have in vain tried to effect; otherwise he can neither enjoy health nor happiness. Tell me in your next letter whether you care about my sending you a large selection of music: you can indeed dispose of what you do not want, and thus repay the expense of the carriage, and have my portrait into the bargain. Say all that is kind and amiable from me to Lorchen, and also to mamma and Christoph. You still have some regard for me? Always rely on the love as well as the friendship of your

BEETHOVEN.

19.

*To Kapellmeister Hofmeister,—Leipzig.*

Vienna, Dec. 15, 1800.

My dear Brother in Art,

I have often intended to answer your proposals, but am frightfully lazy about all correspondence, so it is usually a good while before I can make up my mind to write dry letters instead of music : I have, however, at last forced myself to answer your application. *Pro primo,* I must tell you how much I regret that you, my much loved brother in the science of music, did not give me some hint, so that I might have offered you my Quartetts, as well as many other things that I have now disposed of. But if you are as conscientious, my dear brother, as many other publishers, who grind to death us poor composers, you will know pretty well how to derive ample profit when the works appear. I now briefly state what you can have from me. 1st. A Septett, *per il violino, viola, violoncello, contra-basso, clarinetto, corno, fagotto ;—tutti obbligati* (I can write nothing that is not *obbligato,* having come into the world with an *obbligato* accompaniment !). This Septett

---

* The letters to Hofmeister, formerly of Vienna, who conducted the correspondence with Beethoven in the name of the firm of 'Hofmeister & Kühnel, Bureau de Musique,' are given here as they first appeared in 1837 in the 'Neue Zeitschrift für Musik.' On applying to the present representative of that firm, I was told that those who now possess these letters decline giving them out of their own hands, and that no copyist can be found able to decipher or transcribe them correctly.

pleases very much. For more general use it might be arranged for one more *violino, viola,* and *violoncello,* instead of the three wind-instruments, *fagotto, clari-netto,* and *corno.\** 2nd. A Grand Symphony with full orchestra [the 1st]. 3rd. A pianoforte Concerto [Op. 19], which I by no means assert to be one of my best, any more than the one Mollo is to publish here [Op. 15], (this is for the benefit of the Leipzig critics!), because *I reserve the best for myself* till I set off on my travels; still the work will not disgrace you to publish. 4th. A Grand Solo Sonata [Op. 22]. These are all I can part with at this moment; a little later you can have a Quintett for stringed instruments, and probably some Quartetts also, and other pieces that I have not at present beside me. In your answer you can yourself fix the prices, and as you are neither an *Italian* nor a *Jew,* nor am I either, we shall no doubt quickly agree. Farewell, and rest assured,

My dear brother in art, of the esteem of your

BEETHOVEN.

## 20.

### *To Kapellmeister Hofmeister.*

Vienna, Jan. 15 (or thereabouts), 1801.

I read your letter, dear brother and friend, with much pleasure, and I thank you for your good opinion of me

---

\* This last phrase is not in the copy before me, but in Marx's 'Biography,' who appears to have seen the original.

and of my works, and hope I may continue to deserve it. I also beg you to present all due thanks to Herr K. [Kühnel] for his politeness and friendship towards me. I, on my part, rejoice in your undertakings, and am glad that when works of art do turn out profitable, they fall to the share of true artists, rather than to that of mere tradesmen.

Your intention to publish Sebastian Bach's works really gladdens my heart, which beats with devotion for the lofty and grand productions of this our father of the science of harmony, and I trust I shall soon see them appear. I hope when golden peace is proclaimed, and your subscription list opened, to procure you many subscribers here.*

With regard to our own transactions, as you wish to know my proposals, they are as follows. I offer you at present the following works :—The Septett (which I already wrote to you about), 20 ducats ; Symphony, 20 ducats ; Concerto, 10 ducats ; Grand Solo Sonata, *allegro, adagio, minuetto, rondo*, 20 ducats. This Sonata [Op. 22] is well up to the mark, my dear brother!

Now for explanations. You may perhaps be surprised that I make no difference of price between the Sonata, Septett, and Symphony. I do so because I find that a Septett or a Symphony has not so great a

---

* I have at this moment in my hands this edition of Bach, bound in one thick volume, together with the first part of Nägeli's edition of the 'Wohltemperirtes Clavier,' also three books of exercises (D, G, and C minor), the 'Toccata in D Minor,' and 'Twice Fifteen Inventions.'

sale as a Sonata, though a Symphony ought unques-
tionably to be of the most value. (N.B. The Septett
consists of a short introductory *adagio*, an *allegro*,
*adagio*, *minuetto*, *andante* with variations, *minuetto*,
and another short *adagio* preceding a *presto*). I only
ask 10 ducats for the Concerto, for, as I already wrote to
you, I do not consider it one of my best. I cannot think
that, taken as a whole, you will consider these prices
exorbitant; at least, I have endeavoured to make them
as moderate as possible for you.

With regard to the banker's draft, as you give me
my choice, I beg you will make it payable by Germüller
or Schüller. The entire sum for the four works will
amount to 70 ducats: I understand no currency but
Vienna ducats, so how many dollars in gold they make
in your money is no affair of mine, for really I am a
very bad man of business and accountant. Now this
*troublesome* business is concluded;—I call it so, heartily
wishing that it could be otherwise here below! There
ought to be only one grand depôt of art in the world, to
which the artist might repair with his works, and on
presenting them receive what he required; but as it
now is, one must be half a tradesman besides—and
how is this to be endured? Good heavens! I may well
call it *troublesome*!

As for the Leipzig oxen,* let them talk!—they cer-

---

* It is thus that Schindler supplies the gap. It is probably an
allusion to the 'Allgemeine Musikalische Zeitung,' founded about three
years previously.

tainly will make no man immortal by their prating, and as little can they deprive of immortality those whom Apollo destines to attain it.

Now may Heaven preserve you and your colleagues! I have been unwell for some time, so it is rather difficult for me at present to write even music, much more letters. I trust we shall have frequent opportunities to assure each other how truly you are my friend, and I yours.

I hope for a speedy answer. Adieu!

L. v. BEETHOVEN.

## 21.

### To Herr Hofmeister.

Vienna, April 22, 1801.

You have indeed too good cause to complain not a little of me. My excuse is that I have been ill, and in addition had so much to do, that I could scarcely even think of what I was to send you. Moreover, the only thing in me that resembles a genius is, that my papers are never in very good order, and yet no one but myself can succeed in arranging them. For instance, in the score of the Concerto, the piano part, according to my usual custom, was not yet written down, so, owing to my hurry, you will receive it in my own very illegible writing. In order that the works may follow as nearly as possible in their proper order, I have marked the numbers to be placed on each, as follows :—

Solo Sonata, Op. 22.
Symphony, Op. 21.
Septett, Op. 20.
Concerto, Op. 19.

I will send you their various titles shortly.

Put me down as a subscriber to Sebastian Bach's works [see Letter 20], and also Prince Lichnowsky. The arrangement of Mozart's Sonatas as Quartetts will do you much credit, and no doubt be profitable also. I wish I could contribute more to the promotion of such an undertaking, but I am an irregular man, and too apt, even with the best intentions, to forget everything; I have, however, mentioned the matter to various people, and I everywhere find them well disposed towards it. It would be a good thing if you would arrange the Septett you are about to publish as a Quintett, with a flute part, for instance; this would be an advantage to amateurs of the flute, who have already importuned me on the subject, and who would swarm round it like insects, and banquet on it.

Now to tell you something of myself. I have written a ballet ['Prometheus'], in which the ballet-master has not done his part so well as might be. The F—— von L—— has also bestowed on us a production which by no means corresponds with the ideas of his genius conveyed by the newspaper reports. F—— seems to have taken Herr M—— [Wenzel Müller ?] as his ideal at the Kusperle, yet without even rising to his level. Such are the fine prospects for us poor people who strive to struggle upwards! My dear friend, pray lose no time in bringing the work before the notice of the public, and write to me soon, that I may know whether by my delay I have entirely forfeited your confidence for the future. Say all that is civil and kind to your partner, Kühnel. Everything shall henceforth be sent finished, and in quick succession. So now farewell, and continue your regards for

Your friend and brother,

BEETHOVEN.

22.

*To Herr Hofmeister.*

Vienna, June, 1801.

I am rather surprised at the communication you have desired your business agent here to make to me; I may well feel offended at your believing me capable of so mean a trick. It would have been a very different thing had I sold my works to rapacious shopkeepers, and then secretly made another good speculation; but, from *one artist to another*, it is rather a strong measure to suspect me of such a proceeding! The whole thing seems to be either a device to put me to the test, or a mere suspicion. In any event I may tell you that

before you received the Septett from me I had sent it
to Mr. Salomon in London (to be played at his own
concert, which I did solely from friendship), with the
express injunction to beware of its getting into other
hands, as it was my intention to have it engraved in
Germany, and, if you choose, you can apply to him for
the confirmation of this. But to give you a further
proof of my integrity, 'I herewith give you the faithful
assurance that I have neither sold the Septett, the
Symphony, the Concerto, nor the Sonata to anyone but
to Messrs. Hofmeister and Kühnel, and that they may
consider them to be their own exclusive property. And
to this I pledge my honour.' You may make what use
you please of this guarantee.

Moreover, I believe Salomon to be as incapable of
the baseness of engraving the Septett as I am of sell-
ing it to him. I was so scrupulous in the matter, that
when applied to by various publishers to sanction a
pianoforte arrangement of the Septett, I at once declined, though I do not even know whether you proposed
making use of it in this way. Here follow the long-
promised titles of the works. There will no doubt
be a good deal to alter and to amend in them; but this
I leave to you. I shall soon expect a letter from you,
and, I hope, the works likewise, which I wish to see
engraved, as others have appeared, and are about to
appear, in connection with these numbers. I look on
your statement as founded on mere rumours, which you

have believed with too much facility, or based entirely
on supposition, induced by having perchance heard that
I had sent the work to Salomon; I cannot, therefore,
but feel some coolness towards such a credulous friend,
though I still subscribe myself

Your friend,

BEETHOVEN.

### 23.

#### *Dedication to Dr. Schmidt.*\*

1801.

Monsieur!

Je sens parfaitement bien, que la Celebrité de Votre
nom ainsi que l'amitié dont Vous m'honorez, exigeroient
de moi la dédicace d'un bien plus important ouvrage.
La seule chose qui a pu me déterminer à Vous offrir
celui-ci de préférence, c'est qu'il me paroît d'une exécu-
tion plus facile et par là même plus propre à contribuer
à la Satisfaction dont Vous jouissez dans l'aimable
Cercle de Votre Famille. — C'est surtout, lorsque les
heureux talents d'une fille chérie se seront developpés
davantage, que je me flatte de voir ce but atteint.
Heureux si j'y ai réussi et si dans cette faible marque
de ma haute estime et de ma gratitude Vous recon-
noissez toute la vivacité et la cordialité de mes sentiments.

LOUIS VAN BEETHOVEN.

\* Grand Trio, Op. 38.

### 24.

*To his Scholar, Ferdinand Ries.**

1801.

Dear Ries,

I send you herewith the four parts corrected by me; please compare the others already written out with these. I also enclose a letter to Count Browne. I have told him that he must make an advance to you of 50 ducats, to enable you to get your outfit. This is absolutely necessary, so it cannot offend him; for after being equipped, you are to go with him to Baden on the Monday of the ensuing week. I must, however, reproach you for not having had recourse to me long ago. Am I not your true friend? Why did you conceal your necessities from me? No friend of mine shall ever be in need, so long as I have anything myself. I would already have sent you a small sum, did I not rely on Browne; if he fails us, then apply at once to your

BEETHOVEN.

### 25.

*To Herr Hofmeister,—Leipzig.*

Vienna, April 8, 1802.

Do you mean to go post-haste to the devil, gentlemen, by proposing that I should write *such a Sonata*?

* Ries names 1801 as the date of this letter, and it was no doubt during that summer that Count Browne was in Baden. Ries' father had assisted the Beethoven family in every way in his power at the time of the mother's death.

During the revolutionary fever, a thing of the kind might have been appropriate, but now, when everything is falling again into the beaten track, and Buonaparte has concluded a *Concordat* with the Pope—such a Sonata as this? If it were a *missa pro Sancta Maria à tre voci*, or a *vesper*, &c., then I would at once take up my pen and write a *credo in unum*, in gigantic semibreves. But, good heavens! such a Sonata, in this fresh dawning Christian epoch. No, no!—it won't do, and I will have none of it.

Now for my answer in quickest *tempo*. The lady can have a Sonata from me, and I am willing to adopt the general outlines of her plan in an *esthetical* point of view, without adhering to the keys named. The price to be 5 ducats: for this sum she can keep the work a year for her own amusement, without either of us being entitled to publish it. After the lapse of a year, the Sonata to revert to me—that is, I can and will then publish it, when, if she considers it any distinction, she may request me to dedicate it to her.

I now, gentlemen, commend you to the grace of God. My Sonata [Op. 22] is well engraved, but you have been a fine time about it! I hope you will usher my Septett into the world a little quicker, as the P—— is waiting for it, and you know the Empress has it; and when there are in this Imperial city people like ——, I cannot be answerable for the result, so lose no time!

Herr —— [Mollo?] has lately published my Quartetts

[Op. 18] full of faults and *errata*, both large and small, which swarm in them like fish in the sea—that is, they are innumerable.  *Questo è un piacere per un autore*— this is what I call engraving [*stechen*, stinging] with a vengeance.* In truth, my skin is a mass of punctures and scratches from this fine edition of my Quartetts! Now farewell, and think of me as I do of you.   Till death, your faithful

L. v. BEETHOVEN.

26.†

*To my Brothers Carl and Johann Beethoven.*

Heiligenstadt, Oct. 6, 1802.

Oh! ye who think or declare me to be hostile, morose, and misanthropical, how unjust you are, and how little you know the secret cause of what appears thus to you! My heart and mind were ever from childhood prone to the most tender feelings of affection, and I was always disposed to accomplish something great.   But you must remember that six years ago I was attacked by an in- curable malady, aggravated by unskilful physicians, deluded from year to year, too, by the hope of relief,

---

* In reference to the musical piracy at that time very prevalent in Austria.

† This beautiful letter I regret not to have seen in the original, it being in the possession of the violin *virtuoso* Ernst, in London.   I have adhered to the version given in the Leipzig 'Allgemeine Musikalische Zeitung,' Oct. 1827.

and at length forced to the conviction of a *lasting affliction* (the cure of which may go on for years, and perhaps after all prove impracticable).

Born with a passionate and excitable temperament, keenly susceptible to the pleasures of society, I was yet obliged early in life to isolate myself, and to pass my existence in solitude. If I at any time resolved to surmount all this, oh! how cruelly was I again repelled by the experience, sadder than ever, of my defective hearing!—and yet I found it impossible to say to others: Speak louder, shout! for I am deaf! Alas! how could I proclaim the deficiency of a sense which ought to have been more perfect with me than with other men—a sense which I once possessed in the highest perfection, to an extent, indeed, that few of my profession ever enjoyed! Alas! I cannot do this! Forgive me therefore when you see me withdraw from you with whom I would so gladly mingle. My misfortune is doubly severe from causing me to be misunderstood. No longer can I enjoy recreation in social intercourse, refined conversation, or mutual outpourings of thought. Completely isolated, I only enter society when compelled to do so. I must live like an exile. In company I am assailed by the most painful apprehensions, from the dread of being exposed to the risk of my condition being observed. It was the same during the last six months I spent in the country. My intelligent physician recommended me to spare my hearing as much as possible, which was

quite in accordance with my present disposition, though
sometimes, tempted by my natural inclination for society, I allowed myself to be beguiled into it. But what
humiliation when anyone beside me heard a flute in
the far distance, while I heard *nothing,* or when others
heard *a shepherd singing,* and I still heard *nothing!*
Such things brought me to the verge of desperation,
and well nigh caused me to put an end to my life.
*Art! art* alone, deterred me. Ah! how could I possibly quit the world before bringing forth all that
I felt it was my vocation to produce? * And thus I
spared this miserable life—so utterly miserable that any
sudden change may reduce me at any moment from
my best condition into the worst. It is decreed that I
must now choose *Patience* for my guide! This I have
done. I hope the resolve will not fail me, steadfastly to
persevere till it may please the inexorable Fates to cut
the thread of my life. Perhaps I may get better, perhaps not. I am prepared for either. Constrained to become a philosopher in my twenty-eighth year! † This is
no slight trial, and more severe on an artist than on anyone else. God looks into my heart, He searches it, and
knows that love for man and feelings of benevolence

---

* A large portion of the 'Eroica' was written in the course of this
summer, but not completed till August 1804.

† Beethoven did not at that time know in what year he was born.
See the subsequent letter of May 2, 1810. He was then far advanced
in his thirty-third year.

have their abode there! Oh! ye who may one day
read this, think that you have done me injustice, and
let anyone similarly afflicted be consoled, by finding
one like himself, who, in defiance of all the obstacles of
nature, has done all in his power to be included in the
ranks of estimable artists and men. My brothers Carl
and Johann, as soon as I am no more, if Professor
Schmidt [see Nos. 18 and 23] be still alive, beg him in
my name to describe my malady, and to add these pages
to the analysis of my disease, that at least, so far as
possible, the world may be reconciled to me after my
death. I also hereby declare you both heirs of my
small fortune (if so it may be called). Share it fairly,
agree together and assist each other. You know that
anything you did to give me pain has been long forgiven. I thank you, my brother Carl in particular, for
the attachment you have shown me of late. My wish
is that you may enjoy a happier life, and one more free
from care, than mine has been. Recommend *Virtue* to
your children; that alone, and not wealth, can ensure
happiness. I speak from experience. It was *Virtue*
alone which sustained me in my misery; I have to
thank her and Art for not having ended my life by
suicide. Farewell! Love each other. I gratefully
thank all my friends, especially Prince Lichnowsky
and Professor Schmidt. I wish one of you to keep
Prince L.'s —— instruments; but I trust this will give
rise to no dissension between you. If you think it

more beneficial, however, you have only to dispose of them. How much I shall rejoice if I can serve you even in the grave! So be it then! I joyfully hasten to meet Death. If he comes before I have had the opportunity of developing all my artistic powers, then, notwithstanding my cruel fate, he will come too early for me, and I should wish for him at a more distant period; but even then I shall be content, for his advent will release me from a state of endless suffering. Come when he may, I shall meet him with courage. Farewell! Do not quite forget me, even in death : I deserve this from you, because during my life I so often thought of you, and wished to make you happy. Amen!

LUDWIG VAN BEETHOVEN.

(Written on the outside.)

Thus, then, I take leave of you, and with sadness too. The fond hope I brought with me here, of being to a certain degree cured, now utterly forsakes me. As autumn leaves fall and wither, so are my hopes blighted. Almost as I came, I depart. Even the lofty courage that so often animated me in the lovely days of summer is gone for ever. Oh, Providence! vouchsafe me one day of pure felicity! How long have I been estranged from the glad echo of true joy! When! oh, my God! when shall I again feel it in the temple of nature and of man?—never? Ah! that would be too hard!

*(Outside.)*

To be read and fulfilled after my death by my brothers Carl and Johann.

## 27.

*Notice.*

November 1802.

I owe it to the public and to myself to state that the
two Quintetts in C and E flat major—one of these
(arranged from a Symphony of mine) published by
Herr Mollo in Vienna, and the other (taken from my
Septett, Op. 20) by Herr Hofmeister in Leipzig—are not
original Quintetts, but only versions of the aforesaid
works given by the publishers. Arrangements in these
days (so fruitful in—arrangements) an author will
find it vain to contend against; but we may at least
justly demand that the fact should be mentioned in
the title-page, neither to injure the reputation of the
author nor to deceive the public. This notice is given
to prevent anything of the kind in future. I also beg
to announce that shortly a new original Quintett of my
composition, in C major, Op. 29, will appear at Breitkopf
& Härtel's in Leipzig.

LUDWIG VAN BEETHOVEN.

## 28.

### To Ferdinand Ries.

Summer of 1803.

You no doubt are aware that I am here. Go to Stein, and ask if he can send me an instrument, on hire. I am afraid of bringing mine here. Come to me this evening about seven o'clock. I lodge in Oberdöbling, on the left side of the street, No. 4, going down the hill towards Heiligenstadt.

## 29.

### To Herr Hofmeister,—Leipzig.

Vienna, Sept. 22, 1803.

I hereby declare all the works you have ordered to be your property. The list of these shall be made out and sent to you with my signature, as the proof of their being your own. I also agree to accept the sum of fifty ducats for them. Are you satisfied?

Perhaps, instead of the variations with violoncello and violin,* I may send you variations for the piano, arranged as a Duett on a song of mine; but Goethe's poetry must also be engraved, as I wrote these variations in an album, and consider them better than the others. Are you satisfied?

---

\* These are the six variations in D, on the air 'Ich denke Dein,' written in 1800 in the album of the Countesses Josephine Deym and Thérèse of Brunswick.

The arrangements are not by me, though I have revised and much improved various passages; but I do not wish you to say that I have arranged them, for it would be false, and I have neither time nor patience to do so. Are you satisfied?

Now farewell! I sincerely wish that all may go well with you. I would gladly make you a present of all my works, if I could do so and still get on in the world; but—remember most people are provided for, and know what they have to live on, while, good heavens! where can an appointment be found at the Imperial Court for such a *parvum talentum com ego*?

Your friend,

L. V. BEETHOVEN.

### 30.

### *Caution.*

November, 1803.

Herr Carl Zulehner, a piratical engraver in Mayence, has announced an edition of my collected works for the pianoforte and also stringed instruments. I consider it my duty publicly to inform all friends of music that I have no share whatever in this edition.

I would never have in any way authorised any collection of my works (which, moreover, I consider premature) without previously consulting the publishers of single pieces, and ensuring that correctness in which editions of my individual works are so deficient. I must also observe that this illegal edition cannot be complete, as several new works of mine are shortly to appear in Paris, and these Herr Zulehner, being a French subject, dare not pirate. I intend to take another opportunity of enumerating the details of the collection of my works to be brought out under my own auspices and careful revision.

LUDWIG VAN BEETHOVEN.

## 31.

### To Herr Ries.*

1804.

Be so good as to make out a list of the mistakes and send it at once to Simrock, and say that the work must appear as soon as possible. I will send him the Sonata [Op. 47] and the Concerto the day after to-morrow.

BEETHOVEN.

## 32.

### To Herr Ries.

I must again ask you to undertake the disagreeable task of making a fair copy of the errors in the Zurich Sonata. I have got your list of *errata* ' *auf der Wieden.*'

---

* Ries relates that the three following notes refer to the pianoforte Sonata, Op. 31, No. 1, carefully engraved by Nägeli in Zurich, which Beethoven consequently sent forthwith to Simrock in Bonn, desiring him to bring out ' *une édition très-correcte*' of the work. He also states that Beethoven was residing in Heiligenstadt at the time the work was first sent [see No. 26]. In Nottebohm's 'Skizzenbuch von Beethoven' he says (p. 43) that the first notice of the appearance of this Sonata was on May 21st, 1803; but Simrock writes to me that the date of the document making over the Sonata to him is 1804.

### 33.

*To Herr Ries.*

Dear Ries,

The signs are wrongly marked, and many of the notes misplaced; so be careful! or your labour will be vain.   *Ch' a detto l' amato bene?*

### 34.

*To Herr Ries.*

Dear Ries,

May I beg you to be so obliging as to copy this *andante* [in the Kreuzer Sonata] for me, however indifferently?   I must send it off to-morrow, and as Heaven alone knows what its fate may then be, I wish to get it transcribed.   But I must have it back to-morrow about one o'clock.   The cause of my troubling you is that one of my copyists is already very much occupied with various things of importance, and the other is ill.

### 35.

*To the Composer Leidesdorf,—Vienna.*\*

Dorf des Leides [village of sorrow—Leidesdorf],

Let the bearer of this, Herr Ries, have some easy Duetts, and, better still, let him have them for nothing. Conduct yourself in accordance with the reformed doctrines.   Farewell!

BEETHOVEN

*Minimus.*

\* Date unknown.   Leidesdorf was also a musicseller.

## 36.

### *To Herr Ries.*

Baden, July 14, 1804.

Dear Ries,

If you can find me better lodgings, I shall be very glad. Tell my brothers not to engage these at once; I have a great desire to get one in a spacious, quiet square or on the Bastei. It is really inexcusable in my brother not to have provided wine, as it is so beneficial and necessary to me. I shall take care to be present at the rehearsal on Wednesday. I am not pleased to hear that it is to be at Schuppanzigh's. He may well be grateful to me if my impertinences make him thinner! Farewell, dear Ries! We have bad weather here, and I am not safe from visitors, so I must take flight in order to be alone.

Your true friend,

L. v. BEETHOVEN.

## 37.

### *To Herr Ries.*

Baden, July 1804.

Dear Ries,

As Breuning [see Nos. 13, 14, and 18] by his conduct has not scrupled to display my character to you and the house-steward as that of a mean, petty, base man, I beg you will convey my reply at once in person to Breuning. I answer only one point, the first in his letter, and I do so solely because it is the only mode of justifying myself in your eyes. Say also to him that I had no intention of reproaching him on account of the delay of the notice to quit, and even if Breuning were really to blame for this, our harmonious relations are so dear and precious in my sight, that, for the sake of a few hundreds more or less, I would never subject any friend of mine to vexation. You are aware, indeed, that I jestingly accused you as the cause of the notice arriving too late. I am quite sure that you must remember this. I had entirely forgotten the whole matter, but at dinner my brother began to say that he thought Breuning was to blame in the affair, which I at once denied, saying that you were in fault. I think this shows plainly enough that I attributed no blame to Breuning; but on this he sprang up like a madman, and insisted on sending for the house-steward. Such behaviour, in the presence of all those with whom I usually associate, and to which I am wholly unaccustomed, caused me to lose all self-control, so I also started up, upset my chair, left the room, and did not return. This conduct induced Breuning to place me in a pretty light to you and the house-steward, and also to send me a letter which I only answered by silence. I have not another word to say to Breuning. His mode of thinking and of acting, with regard to me, proves that there never ought to have been such friendly intimacy between us, and assuredly it can never more be restored. I wished to make you acquainted with this, as your version of the occurrence degraded both my words and actions. I know that, had you been aware of the real state of the affair, you would not have said what you did, and with this I am satisfied.

I now beg of you, dear Ries, to go to my brother, the apothecary, as soon as you receive this letter, and say to him that I mean to leave Baden in the course of a few days, and that he is to engage the lodging in Döbling as soon as you have given him this message. I had nearly left this to-day; I detest being here—I am sick of it. For Heaven's sake urge him to close the bargain at once, for I want to take possession immediately. Neither show nor speak to anyone of what is written in the previous page of this letter: I wish to prove to him in every respect that I am not so meanly disposed as he is. Indeed I have written to him, although my resolve as to the dissolution of our friendship remains firm and unchangeable.

Your friend,<br>
BEETHOVEN.

38.

*To Herr Ries.*

Berlin, July 24, 1804.

. . . You were no doubt not a little surprised about the affair with Breuning; believe me, my dear friend, that the ebullition on my part was only an outbreak caused by many previous scenes of a disagreeable nature. I have the gift of being able to conceal and to repress my susceptibility on many occasions, but if attacked at a time when I chance to be peculiarly irritable, I burst forth more violently than anyone. Breuning certainly possesses many admirable qualities, but he thinks himself quite faultless, whereas the very defects that he discovers in others are those which he possesses himself to the highest degree. From my childhood I have always despised his petty mind. My powers of discrimination enabled me to foresee the result with Breuning, for our modes of thinking, acting, and feeling are entirely opposite; and yet I believed that these difficulties might be overcome, but experience has disproved this. So now I want no more of his friendship! I have only found two friends in the world with whom I never had a misunderstanding; but what men these were! One is dead, the other still lives. Although for nearly six years past we have seen nothing of each other, yet I know that I still hold the first place in his heart, as he does in mine [see No. 12]. The true basis of friendship is to be found in sympathy of heart and soul. I only wish you could have read the letter I wrote to Breuning, and his to me. No! never can he be restored to his former place in my heart. The man who could attribute to his friend so base a mode of thinking, and could himself have recourse to so base a mode of acting towards him, is no longer worthy of my friendship.

Do not forget the affair of my apartments. Fare-

well! Do not be too much addicted to tailoring,* remember me to the fairest of the fair, and send me half
a dozen needles.

I never could have believed that I could be so idle
as I am here. If this be followed by a fit of industry,
something worth while may be produced.

*Vale!*

Your BEETHOVEN.

39.

*To Messrs. Artaria & Co.*†

Vienna, June 1, 1805.

I must inform you that the affair about the new
Quintett is settled between Count Fries and myself.

The Count has just assured me that he intends to
make you a present of it; it is too late to-day for a
written agreement on the subject, but one shall be sent
early in the ensuing week. This intelligence must suf-
fice for the present, and I think I at all events deserve
your thanks for it.

Your obedient servant,

LUDWIG VAN BEETHOVEN.

---

* Ries says, in Wegeler's 'Biographical Notices' :—'Beethoven never
visited me more frequently than when I lived in the house of a tailor,
with three very handsome but thoroughly respectable daughters.'

† The Quintett is probably not that in C, Op. 29, dedicated to Count
v. Fries, previously published in 1803 by Breitkopf & Härtel [see
No. 27]. It is more likely that he alludes to a new Quintett which the
Count had no doubt ordered.

## 40.

*To Madame la Princesse Liechtenstein, &c.*\*

November 1805.

Pray pardon me, illustrious Princess, if the bearer of this should cause you an unpleasant surprise. Poor Ries, my scholar, is forced by this unhappy war to shoulder a musket, and must moreover leave this in a few days, being a foreigner. He has nothing, literally nothing, and is obliged to take a long journey. All chance of a concert on his behalf is thus entirely at an end, and he must have recourse to the benevolence of others. I recommend him to you. I know you will forgive the step I have taken. A noble-minded man would only have recourse to such measures in the most utter extremity. Confident of this, I send the poor youth to you, in the hope of somewhat improving his circumstances. He is forced to apply to all who know him.

I am, with the deepest respect, yours,

L. VAN BEETHOVEN.

---

\* Communicated by Ries himself, who, to Beethoven's extreme indignation, did not deliver the note. See Wegeler's work, p. 134. The following remark is added:—' Date unknown; written a few days before the entrance of the French in 1805' (which took place Nov. 13). Ries, a native of Bonn, was now a French subject, and recalled under the laws of conscription. The Sonata, Op. 27, No. 1, is dedicated to Princess Liechtenstein.

## 41.

### To Herr Meyer.*

1805.

Dear Meyer,

Pray try to persuade Herr v. Seyfried to direct my Opera, as I wish on this occasion to see and hear it myself *from a distance* : in this way my patience will at all events not be so severely tried as when I am close enough to hear my music so bungled. I really do believe that it is done on purpose to annoy me ! I will say nothing of the wind-instruments; but all *pp.*'s, *cresc.*, *discresc.*, and all *f.*'s and *ff.*'s may as well be struck out of my Opera, for no attention whatever is paid to them. I shall lose all pleasure in composing anything in future, if I am to hear it given thus. To-morrow or the day after I will come to fetch you to dinner. To-day I am again unwell.

Your friend,

BEETHOVEN.

If the Opera is to be performed the day after to-morrow, there must be another private rehearsal to-morrow, or *each time it will be given worse and worse.*

---

* Meyer, the husband of Mozart's eldest sister-in-law, Josepha (Hofer's widow), sang the part of Pizarro at the first performance of ' Fidelio, Nov. 20, 1805, and also at a later period. Seyfried was at that time Kapellmeister at the Theatre 'an der Wien.'

## 42.

*Testimonial for C. Czerny.*

Vienna, Dec. 7, 1805.

I, the undersigned, am glad to bear testimony to young Carl Czerny having made the most extraordinary progress on the pianoforte, far beyond what might be expected at the age of fourteen.. I consider him deserving of all possible assistance, not only from what I have already referred to, but from his astonishing memory, and more especially from his parents having spent all their means in cultivating the talent of their promising son.

LUDWIG VAN BEETHOVEN.

## 43.

*To Herr Röckel.*[*]

1806.

Dear Röckel,

Be sure that you arrange matters properly with Mdlle. Milder, and say to her previously from me, that I hope she will not sing anywhere else. I intend to call on her to-morrow to kiss the hem of her garment. Do not also forget Marconi, and forgive me for giving you so much trouble..

Yours wholly,

BEETHOVEN.

[*] Röckel, in 1806 tenor at the Theatre 'an der Wien,' sang the part of Florestan in the spring of that year, when 'Fidelio' was revived. Mdlle. Milder, afterwards Mdme. Hauptmann, played Leonore, Mdme. Marconi was also prima donna.

## 44.

### *To Herr Collin,\* Court Secretary and Poet.*

My esteemed Collin,

I hear that you are about to fulfil my greatest wish and your own purpose. Much as I desire to express my delight to you in person, I cannot find time to do so, having so much to occupy me. Pray do not then ascribe this to any˙ want of proper attention towards you. I send you the ' Armida;' as soon as you have entirely done with it, pray return it, as it does not belong to me. I am, with sincere esteem,

Yours,

BEETHOVEN.

## 45.

### *To Herr Gleichenstein.†*

I should like very much, my good Gleichenstein, to speak to you this forenoon between one and two o'clock,

---

\* Collin, Court Secretary, was the author of ' Coriolanus,' a tragedy, for which Beethoven in 1807 wrote the celebrated Overture dedicated to that poet. According to Reichardt, Collin offered the libretto of ' Bradamante' to Beethoven in 1808, which Reichardt subsequently composed. This note evidently refers to a *libretto.*

† Probably in reference to a conference with regard to a contract for the publication of his works, Op. 58, 59, 60, 61, and 62, that Beethoven had made on the 20th April, 1807, with Muzio Clementi, who had established a large music firm in London; it was also signed by Baron Gleichen.

Beethoven's first intention was to dedicate Op. 58 to him, which is evident from a large page in Schindler's work, on which is written in or in the afternoon, and where you please. To-day I am too busy to call early enough to find you at home. Give me an answer, and don't forget to appoint the place for us to meet. Farewell, and continue your regard for your

BEETHOVEN.

46.

*To the Directors of the Court Theatre.**

Vienna, December 1807.

The undersigned has cause to flatter himself that during the period of his stay in Vienna he has gained some favour and approbation from the highest nobility, as well as from the public at large, his works having met with an honourable reception both in this and other countries. Nevertheless he has had difficulties of every kind to contend against, and has not hitherto been so fortunate as to acquire a position that would enable him *to live solely for art,* and to develope his talents to a still higher degree of perfection, which ought to be the aim

---

bold characters, by the master's own hand, ' *Quatrième Concerto pour le Piano, avec accompagnement, etc., dédié à son ami Gleichenstein,*' &c. The name of the Archduke Rudolph had been previously written, and was eventually adopted, and Gleichenstein afterwards received the dedication of the Grand Sonata with violoncello, Op. 69.

    * This application was fruitless. See Reichardt's 'Vertraute Briefe.' 'These two (Lobkowitz and Esterhazy) are the heads of the great theatrical direction, which consists entirely of princes and counts, who conduct all the large theatres on their own account and at their own risk.' The close of this letter shows that it was written in December.

of every artist, thus ensuring future independence instead of mere casual profits.

The mere wish *to gain a livelihood* has never been the leading clue that has hitherto guided the undersigned on his path. His great aim has been the *interest of art* and the ennobling of taste, while his genius, soaring to a higher ideal and greater perfection, frequently compelled him to sacrifice his talents and profits to the Muse. Still works of this kind won for him a reputation in distant lands, securing him the most favourable reception in various places of distinction, and a position befitting his talents and acquirements.

The undersigned does not, however, hesitate to say that this city is above all others the most precious and desirable in his eyes, owing to the number of years he has lived here, the favour and approval he has enjoyed from both high and low, and his wish fully to realise the expectations he has had the good fortune to excite, but most of all, he may truly say, from his *patriotism as a German.* Before, therefore, making up his mind to leave a place so dear to him, he begs to refer to a hint which the reigning Prince Lichnowsky was so kind as to give him, to the effect that the directors of the theatre were disposed to engage the undersigned on reasonable conditions in the service of their theatre, and to ensure his remaining in Vienna by securing to him a permanent position, more propitious to the further exercise of his talents. As this assurance is entirely in

accordance with the wishes of the undersigned, he takes
the liberty, with all due respect, to place before the
directors his readiness to enter into such an engagement, and begs to state the following conditions for
their gracious consideration.

1. The undersigned undertakes and pledges himself
to compose each year at least *one Grand Opera*, to be
selected by the directors and himself; in return for this
he demands a *fixed salary* of 2,400 florins a year, and
also a free benefit at the third performance of each such
Opera.

2. He also agrees to supply the directors annually
with a little *Operetta* or a *Divertissement*, with choruses
or occasional music of the kind as may be required,
*gratis*; he feels confident that on the other hand the
directors will not refuse, in return for these various
labours, to grant him *a benefit concert* at all events once
a year in one of the theatres. Surely the above conditions cannot be thought exorbitant or unreasonable,
when the expenditure of time and energy entailed by
the production of an *Opera* is taken into account, as it
entirely excludes the possibility of all other mental
exertion; in other places, too, the author and his
family have a share in the profits of every individual
performance, so that even *one* successful work at once
ensures the future fortunes of the composer. It must
also be considered how prejudicial the present rate of
exchange is to artists here, and likewise the high price

of the necessaries of life, while a residence in foreign countries is open to them.

But in any event, whether the directors accede to or decline this present proposal, the undersigned ventures to request that he may be permitted to give a concert for his own benefit in one of the theatres. For if his conditions be accepted, the undersigned must devote all his time and talents to the composition of such an Opera, and thus be prevented working in any other way for profit. In case of the non-acceptance of these proposals, as the concert he was authorised to give last year did not take place owing to various obstacles, he would entreat, as a parting token of the favour hitherto vouchsafed to him, that the promise of last year may now be fulfilled. In the former case, he would beg to suggest *Annunciation Day* [April 4th] for his concert, and in the latter a day during the ensuing Christmas vacation.

LUDWIG VAN BEETHOVEN, M. P.

[Manu propria.]

47.

*To Count Franz von Oppersdorf.**

Vienna, Nov. 1, 1088 [*sic* !].

My dear Count,

I fear you will look on me with displeasure when I tell you that necessity compelled me not only to dispose

---

* The fourth Symphony is dedicated to Count Oppersdorf.

of the Symphony I wrote for you, but to transfer another also to some one else. Be assured, however, that you shall soon receive the one I intend for you. I hope that both you and the Countess, to whom I beg my kind regards, have been well since we met. I am at this moment staying with Countess Erdödy in the apartments below those of Prince Lichnowsky. I mention this in case you do me the honour to call on me when you are in Vienna. My circumstances are improving, without having recourse to the intervention of people *who treat their friends insultingly.* I have also the offer of being made *Kapellmeister* to the King of Westphalia, and it is possible that I may accept the proposal. Farewell, and sometimes think of your attached friend,

BEETHOVEN.

48.*

I fear I am too late for to-day, but I have only now been able to get back your memorial from C——, because H—— wished to add various items here and there. I do beg of you to dwell chiefly on the great importance to me of adequate opportunities to exercise

---

\* This note, now first published, refers to the call Beethoven had received, mentioned in the previous No. The sketch of the memorial that follows is not, however, in Beethoven's writing, and perhaps not even composed by him [see also No. 46]. It is well known that the Archduke Rudolph, Prince Kinsky, and Prince Lobkowitz had secured to the *maestro* a salary of 4,000 gulden.

my art; by so doing you will write what is most in accordance with my head and my heart. The preamble must set forth what I am to have in Westphalia—-600 ducats in gold, 150 ducats for travelling expenses; all I have to do in return for this sum being to direct the King's [Jerome's] concerts, which are short and few in number. I am not even bound to direct any Opera I may write. So, thus freed from all care, I shall be able to devote myself entirely to the most important object of my art—to write great works. An orchestra is also to be placed at my disposition.

N.B. As member of a theatrical association, the title need not be insisted on, as it can produce nothing but annoyance. With regard to the *Imperial service*, I think that point requires delicate handling, and not less so the solicitation for the title of *Imperial Kapell-meister*. It must, however, be made quite clear that I am to receive a sufficient salary from the Court to enable me to renounce the annuity which I at present receive from the gentlemen in question [the Archduke Rudolph, Prince Kinsky, and Prince Lobkowitz], which I think will be most suitably expressed by my stating that it is my hope, and has ever been my most ardent wish, to enter the Imperial service, when I shall be ready to give up as much of the above salary as the sum I am to receive from His Imperial Majesty amounts to. (N.B. We must have it to-morrow at twelve o'clock, as we go to Kinsky then. I hope to see you to-day).

### 49.

The aim and endeavour of every true artist must be to acquire a position in which he can occupy himself exclusively with the accomplishment of great works, undisturbed by other avocations or by considerations of economy. A composer, therefore, can have no more ardent wish than to devote himself wholly to the creation of works of importance, to be produced before the public. He must also keep in view the prospect of old age, in order to make a sufficient provision for that period.

The King of Westphalia has offered Beethoven a salary of 600 gold ducats for life, and 150 ducats for travelling expenses, in return for which his sole obligations are, occasionally to play before His Majesty, and to conduct his chamber concerts, which are both few and short. This proposal is of a most beneficial nature both to art and the artist.

Beethoven, however, much prefers a residence in this capital, feeling so much gratitude for the many proofs of kindness he has received in it, and so much patriotism for his adopted fatherland, that he will never cease to consider himself an Austrian artist, nor take up his abode elsewhere, if anything approaching to the same advantages are conferred on him here.

As many persons of high, indeed of the very highest rank, have requested him to name the conditions on which he would be disposed to remain here, in compliance with their wish he states as follows :—

1. Beethoven must receive from some influential nobleman security for a permanent salary for life: various persons of consideration might contribute to make up the amount of this salary, which, at the present increased price of all commodities, must not consist of less than 4,000 florins *per annum.* Beethoven's wish is that the donors of this sum should be considered as co-operating in the production of his future great works, by thus enabling him to devote himself entirely to these labours, and by relieving him from all other occupations.

2. Beethoven must always retain the privilege of travelling in the interests of art, for in this way alone can he make himself known, and acquire some fortune.

3. His most ardent desire and eager wish is to be received into the Imperial service, when such an appointment would enable him partly or wholly to renounce the proposed salary. In the meantime the title of *Imperial Kapellmeister* would be very gratifying to him; and if this wish could be realised, the value of his abode here would be much enhanced in his eyes.

If his desire be fulfilled, and a salary granted by His Majesty to Beethoven, he will renounce so much of the said 4,000 florins as the Imperial salary shall amount to, or if this appointment be 4,000 florins, he will give up the whole of the former sum.

4. As Beethoven wishes from time to time to produce before the public at large his new great works, he
desires an assurance from the present directors of the
theatre on their part, and that of their successors, that
they will authorise him to give a concert for his own
benefit every year on Palm Sunday, in the Theatre ' an
der Wien.' In return for which Beethoven agrees to
arrange and direct an annual concert for the benefit of
the poor, or, if this cannot be managed, at all events to
furnish a new work of his own for such a concert.


### 50.

*To Zmeskall.*

December 1808.

My excellent Friend,

All would go well now if we had only a curtain;
without it the *Aria* ['Ah ! Perfido'] *will be a failure.**
I only heard this to-day from S. [Seyfried], and it
vexes me much : a curtain of any kind will do, even a
bed-curtain, or merely a *kind of gauze screen*, which

---

* Reichardt, in his ' Vertraute Briefe' relates among other things about
the concert given by Beethoven in the Royal Theatre ' an der Wien,'
Oct. 22, 1808, as follows :—' Poor Beethoven, who derived from this
concert the first and only net profits which accrued to him during the
whole year, met with great opposition and very slender support in
arranging and carrying it out. First came ' the Pastoral Symphony, or
Reminiscences of Rural Life ;' then followed, as the sixth piece, a long
Italian *scena*, sung by Demoiselle Killitzky, a lovely Bohemian with a
lovely voice.' The above note [to Zmeskall ?] certainly refers to this
concert.

could be instantly removed. There must be something;
for the Aria is in the *dramatic style,* and better adapted
for the stage than for effect in a concert-room. *Without
a curtain, or something of the sort, the Aria will be
devoid of all meaning, and ruined! ruined! ruined!!
Devil take it all!* The Court will probably be present.
Baron Schweitzer [Chamberlain of the Archduke Anton]
requested me earnestly to make the application myself.
Archduke Carl granted me an audience and promised
to come. The Empress *neither promised nor refused.*

A hanging curtain!!!! or the Aria and I will both
be hanged to-morrow. Farewell! I embrace you as
cordially on this new year as in the old one. *With or
without a curtain!*

Your BEETHOVEN.

## 51.
### To Ferdinand Ries.*

1809.

My dear Fellow,

Your friends have at any rate given you very bad
advice—but I know all about them; they are the very
same to whom you sent that fine news about me from

---

* Ries himself gives the date of this note as 1809, though he cannot
recall what gave rise to it. It is probably connected with a fact mentioned by Wegeler, p. 95, that Reichardt, who was at that time in
Vienna, had advised Beethoven's young pupil, Ries, to apply to the
King of Westphalia for the appointment of Kapellmeister, which he
had recently given up. This was reported to Beethoven, and roused his
ire. Ries, too, had written from Paris that the taste in music there
was very indifferent, that Beethoven's works were little known or played

Paris ; the very same who enquired about my age—
information that you contrived to supply so correctly !
—the very same who have often before injured you in
my opinion, but now permanently.  Farewell !

BEETHOVEN.

## 52.

### To Zmeskall.*

March 7, 1809.

It is just what I expected !  As to the blows, that is
rather far-fetched.  The story is at least three months
old, and very different from what he now makes it out
to be.  The whole stupid affair was caused by a female
huckster and a couple of low fellows.  I lose very little.
He no doubt was corrupted in the very house where I
am now living.

## 53.

### To Zmeskall.

My most excellent, high and well-born Herr v.
Zmeskall, Court Secretary and Member of the Society

in that city.  Beethoven was also very susceptible with regard to his age.
At the request of some of Beethoven's friends, Ries, in 1805, obtained
Beethoven's baptismal certificate, and sent it to Vienna.  But the
*maestro's* wrath on this occasion passed away as quickly as usual.

* [See No. 10.]  The notes to Zmeskall generally have the dates
written by himself.  This one bears the date March 7, 1809.  In all
points connected with domestic life, and especially in household matters
and discords, Zmeskall was always a kind and consolatory friend.
Beethoven at that time lived in the same house with Countess Erdödy.
(See No. 74.)

of the Single Blessed,—If I come to see you to-day, ascribe it to the fact that a person wishes to speak to me at your house whom I could not refuse to see. I come without any *card* from you, but I hope you will not on that account *dis-card* me.

Yours truly—most truly,

L. v. BEETHOVEN.

54.

*To Zmeskall.*

It seems to me, dear Zmeskall, if war really does break out, when it comes to an end you will be the very man for an appointment in the Peace Legation. What a glorious office!!! I leave it entirely to you to do the best you can about my servant, only henceforth Countess Erdödy must not attempt to exercise the smallest influence over him. She says she made him a present of twenty-five florins, and gave him five florins a month, solely to induce him to stay with me. I cannot refuse to believe this trait of generosity, but I do not choose that it should be repeated. Farewell! I thank you for your friendship, and hope soon to see you.

Yours ever,

BEETHOVEN.

## 55.

### *To Zmeskall.**

April 16, 1809.

If I cannot come to-day, dear Zmeskall, which is very possible, ask Baroness von —— [name illegible] to give you the pianoforte part of the Trios, and be so good as to send them and the other parts to me to-day.

In haste,

Your BEETHOVEN.

## 56.

### *To Zmeskall.*

April 17, 1809.

Dear Z.,

A suitable lodging has just been found out for me, but I need some one to help me in the affair. I cannot employ my brother, because he only recommends what costs least money. Let me know, therefore, if we can go together to look at the house. It is in the Klepperstall.†

## 57.

### *To Zmeskall.*

April 25, 1809.

I shall be glad, right glad, to play. I send you the violoncello part; if you find that you can manage it,

---

* April 16, 1809. By the Terzetts he no doubt means the Trios, Op. 70, dedicated to Countess Erdödy.

† An der Mölker Bastei.

play it yourself, or let old Kraft* do so. I will tell you about the lodging when we meet.

Your friend,

BEETHOVEN.

58.

*To Zmeskall.*†

May 14, 1809.

My dear little musical old Count!

I think after all it would be advisable to let old Kraft play, as the Trios are to be heard for the first time (in society), and you can play them afterwards; but I leave it all to your own option. If you meet with any difficulties, one of which may possibly be that Kraft and S. [Schuppanzigh] do not harmonise well together, then Herr v. Zmeskall must distinguish himself not as a mere musical Count, but as an energetic musician.

Your friend,

BEETHOVEN.

---

* Anton Kraft (and likewise his son, Nicolaus Kraft) was a most admirable violoncello-player, with whom Beethoven from the earliest days of his residence in Vienna had played a great deal at Prince Lichnowsky's. Kraft was at that time in Prince Lobkowitz's band.

† Kraft and Schuppanzigh were then each giving Quartett *soirées*.

## 59.

### To Freiherr v. Hammer-Purgstall.*

1809.

I feel almost ashamed of your complaisance and kindness in permitting me to see the MS. of your as yet unknown literary treasures. Pray receive my sincere thanks. I also beg to return both your Operettas. Wholly engrossed by my professional avocations, it is impossible for me to give an opinion, especially with regard to the Indian Operetta; as soon as time permits, I will call on you for the purpose of discussing this subject, and also the Oratorio of 'The Deluge.' Pray always include me among the warm admirers of your great talents.

I am, Sir, with sincere esteem, your obedient

BEETHOVEN.

## 60.

### To Freiherr v. Hammer-Purgstall.†

1809.

Forgive me, my dear H——, for not having brought you the letter for Paris. I have been, and still am, so

---

* I see in Schindler's 'Beethoven,' that he wished to have 'an Indian Chorus of a religious character' from this renowned Orientalist, who in sending his 'Persian Operetta,' written 'rather with an ideal than a musical object,' and likewise an Oratorio, 'The Deluge,' remarks :—'Should you not find these works in all respects executed quite to your taste, still I feel convinced that through the genius of a Beethoven alone can music portray the rising of the great flood and the pacifying of the surging waters.'

† Reichardt states that Stoll was in Vienna in the spring of 1809,

much occupied, that day after day I am obliged to delay writing it, but you shall have it to-morrow, even if I am unable to come myself to see you, which I am most anxious to do.

There is another matter that I would most earnestly press on you; perhaps you might succeed in doing something for a *poor unfortunate man.* I allude to Herr Stoll, son of the celebrated physician. With many persons the question is whether a man has been ruined by his own fault or by that of others, but this is not so with either you or me; it is sufficient that Stoll is unfortunate, and looks on a journey to Paris as his sole resource, having last year made many influential acquaintances, who, when he goes there, are to endeavour to procure him a professorship in Westphalia. Stoll has therefore applied to Herr v. Neumann, in the State Chancery Office, to send him with a government courier to Paris, but the latter refuses to take him for less than 25 Louis d'or. Now I request you, my dear friend, to speak to Herr v. Neumann to arrange, if possible, that the courier should either take Stoll *gratis*, or for a small sum. I am persuaded that if there is nothing particular against it, you will be glad to interest yourself in poor Stoll. I return to the country to-day, but hope soon to be so fortunate as to enjoy an hour of

which fixes the date of this letter. Napoleon bestowed a pension on the young poet (who appears to have gone to Paris), mistaking him for his father, the celebrated physician.

your society. In the meantime I send you my best wishes, and beg you will believe in the sincere esteem of

Your obedient

LUDWIG V. BEETHOVEN.

### 61.

*To Baroness von Drossdick.*

My esteemed Thérèse,

You will receive with this what I promised. Had not many serious obstacles intervened, I would have sent you more, in order to show you that where my friends are concerned *I always perform more than I promise.* I hope, and do not doubt, that you are agreeably occupied and enjoying society, but not too much, I trust, to prevent your thinking of us. It would show too much confidence in you, or too high an estimation of my own merits, were I to attribute the sentiment to you, 'That people are not together only when present, but that the absent and the dead also live with us.' Who could ascribe such a thought to the volatile Thérèse, who takes the world so lightly? Among your various occupations, do not forget the piano, or rather, music in general, for which you have so fine a talent: why not then seriously cultivate it? You, who have so much feeling for the good and the beautiful, should strive to recognise the perfections of so charming an art, which in return always casts so bright a reflection on us.

I live in entire quiet and solitude, and even though occasional flashes of light arouse me, still since you all left this I feel a hopeless void which even my art, usually so faithful to me, has not yet triumphed over. Your pianoforte is ordered, and you shall soon have it. What a difference you must have discovered between the treatment of the Theme I extemporised on the other evening and the mode in which I have recently written it out for you? You must explain this yourself, only do not find the solution in the punch! How happy you are to get away so soon to the country! I cannot enjoy this luxury till the 8th. I look forward to it with the delight of a child. What happiness I shall feel in wandering among groves and woods, and among trees and plants, and rocks! No man on earth can love the country as I do! Thickets, trees, and rocks supply the echo man longs for!

You shall soon receive some more of my compositions, which will not cause you to complain so much of difficulties. Have you read Goethe's 'Wilhelm Meister,' and Schlegel's 'Translations of Shakspeare'? People have so much leisure in the country, that perhaps you would like me to send you these works? It happens that I have an acquaintance in your neighbourhood, so perhaps you may see me some morning early for half an hour, after which I must be off again

You will also observe that I intend to bore you for as short a time as possible.*

Commend me to the regard of your father and mother, though I have as yet no right to claim it. Remember me also to your cousin M. [Mathilde]. Farewell, my esteemed Thérèse ; I wish you all the good and charm that life can offer. Think of me kindly, and forget my follies. Rest assured that no one would more rejoice to hear of your happiness, even were you to feel no interest in your devoted servant and friend,

BEETHOVEN.

N.B. It would be very amiable in you to write me a few lines, to say if I can be of any use to you here.

62.

*A Mdlle. Mdlle. de Gerardi.†*

Dear Mdlle. G.,

I cannot with truth deny that the verses you sent have considerably embarrassed me. It causes a strange

---

* Herr v. Malfatti Rohrenbach, nephew of the renowned physician who was so prominent in Beethoven's last illness, lately related to me in Vienna as follows:—Beethoven went to pay a visit to young Frau Thérèse, Baroness Drossdick, at Mödling, but not finding her at home, he tore a sheet of music-paper out of a book, and wrote some music to a verse of Matthisson's, and on the other side ʟinscribed, in large letters, 'To my dear Thérèse.' The 'Mathilde' mentioned farther on was, according to Bärmann, a Baroness Gleichenstein. [See No. 45.]

† Nothing has hitherto been ascertained respecting either the date of this note, or the lady to whom it is addressed.

sensation to see and hear yourself praised, and yet to be conscious of your own defects, as I am. I consider such occurrences as mere incitements to strive to draw nearer the unattainable goal set before us by art and nature, difficult as it may be. These verses are truly beautiful, with the exception of one fault that we often find in poets, which is, their being misled by Fancy to believe that they really do see and hear *what they wish to see and hear*, and yet even this is far below their ideal. You may well believe that I wish to become acquainted with the poet or poetess; pray receive also yourself my thanks for the kindly feeling you show towards your sincere friend,

L. v. BEETHOVEN.

## 63.

### *To Zmeskall.**

January 23, 1810.

What are you about? My gaiety yesterday, though only assumed, has not only vexed but offended you. The *uninvited guests* seemed so little to deserve your ill humour, that I endeavoured to use all my friendly influence to prevent your giving way to it, by my pretended flow of spirits. I am still suffering from indigestion. Say whether you can meet me at the 'Swan' to-day.

Your true friend,<br>BEETHOVEN.

---

* The cause that gave rise to this note is not known.

64.

*To Wegeler.*

My dear old Friend,

These lines may very possibly cause you some surprise, and yet, though you have no written proof of it, I always retain the most lively remembrance of you. Among my MSS. is one that has long been destined for you, and which you shall certainly receive this summer. For the last two years my secluded and quiet life has been at an end, and I have been forcibly drawn into the vortex of the world; though as yet I have attained no good result from this—nay, perhaps rather the reverse—but who has not been affected by the storms around us? Still I should not only be happy, but the happiest of men, if a demon had not taken up his settled abode in my ears. Had I not somewhere read that man must not voluntarily put an end to his life while he can still perform even one good deed, I should long since have been no more, and by my own hand too! Ah! how fair is life; but for me it is for ever poisoned!

You will not refuse me one friendly service, which is to procure me my baptismal certificate. As Steffen Breuning has an account with you, he can pay any expenses you may incur, and I will repay him here. If you think it worth while to make the enquiry in person, and choose to make a journey from Coblenz to Bonn, you have only to charge it all to me. I must, however, warn you that I had an *elder brother* whose name was also Ludwig, with the second name of *Maria*, who died. In order to know my precise age, the date of my birth must be first ascertained, this circumstance having already led others into error, and caused me to be thought older than I really am. Unluckily, I lived for some time without myself knowing my age [see Nos. 26 and 51]. I had a book containing all family incidents, but it has been lost, Heaven knows how! So pardon my urgently requesting you to try to discover *Ludwig Maria's* birth, as well as that of the present Ludwig. The sooner you can send me the certificate of baptism the more obliged shall I be.* I am told that you sing one of my songs in your Freemason Lodge, probably the one in E major, which I have not myself got; send it to me, and I promise to compensate you threefold and fourfold.† Think of me with kindness, little as I apparently deserve it. Embrace your dear wife and children, and all whom you love, in the name of your friend,

BEETHOVEN.

---

\* Wegeler says:—' I discovered the solution of the enigma (why the baptismal certificate was so eagerly sought) from a letter written to me three months afterwards by my brother-in-law, Stephan von Breuning, in which he said: "Beethoven tells me at least once a week that he means to write to you; but I believe his *intended marriage is broken off*, he therefore feels no ardent inclination to thank you for having procured his baptismal certificate." '

† Beethoven was mistaken; Wegeler had only supplied other music to the words of Matthisson's 'Opfer Lied.'

## 65.

### To Zmeskall.

July 9, 1810.

Dear Z.,

You are about to travel, and so am I on account of my health. In the meantime all goes topsy-turvy with me. The *Herr** wants to have me with him, and Art is not less urgent in her claims. I am partly in Schönbrunn and partly here; every day assailed by messages from strangers and new acquaintances, and even as regards art I am often driven nearly distracted by my undeserved fame. Fortune seeks me, and for that very reason I almost dread some new calamity. As for your *Iphigénie,* the facts are these. I have not seen it for the last two years and a half, and have no doubt lent it to some one; but to whom?—that is the question. I have sent in all directions, and have not yet discovered it, but hope still to find it. If lost, you shall be indemnified. Farewell, my dear Z.! I trust that when we meet again you will find that my art has made some progress in the interim.

Ever remain my friend, as much as I am yours,

BEETHOVEN.

* The 'Herr' is his pupil, the Archduke Rudolph.

## 66.

### *To Bettina Brentano.*[*]

Vienna, August 11, 1810.

My dearest Friend,

Never was there a lovelier spring than this year; I say so, and feel it too, because it was then I first knew

---

[*] The celebrated letters to Bettina are given here exactly as published in her book 'Ilius Pamphilius und die Ambrosia' (Berlin, Arnim, 1857) in two volumes. I never myself had any doubts of their being genuine (with the exception of perhaps some words in the middle of the third letter), nor can anyone now distrust them, especially after the publication of 'Beethoven's Letters.' But for the sake of those for whom the weight of innate conviction is not sufficient proof, I may here mention that in December 1864, Professor Moritz Carrière, in Munich, when conversing with me about 'Beethoven's Letters,' expressly assured me that these three letters were genuine, and that he had seen them in Berlin at Bettina v. Arnim's in 1839, and read them most attentively and with the deepest interest. From their important contents, he urged their immediate publication; and when this shortly after ensued, no change whatever struck him as having been made in the original text; on the contrary, he still perfectly remembered that the much-disputed phraseology (and especially the incident with Goethe) was precisely the same as in the originals. This testimony seems to me the more weighty, as M. Carrière must not in such matters be looked on as a novice, but as a competent judge, who has carefully studied all that concerns our literary heroes, and who would not permit anything to be falsely imputed to Beethoven any more than to Goethe. Beethoven's biography is, however, the proper place to discuss more closely such things, especially his character and his conduct in this particular case. At present we only refer in general terms to the first chapter of 'Beethoven's Jugend,' which gives all the facts connected with these letters to Bettina and the following ones—a characteristic likeness of Beethoven thus impressed itself on the mind of the biographer, and was reproduced in a few bold outlines in his 'Biography.' These letters could not, however, possibly be given *in extenso* in a general introduction to a comprehensive biography.

you. You have yourself seen that in society I am like a fish on the sand, which writhes, and writhes, but cannot get away till some benevolent Galatea casts it back into the mighty ocean. I was indeed fairly stranded, dearest friend, when surprised by you at a moment in which moroseness had entirely mastered me; but how quickly it vanished at your aspect! I was at once conscious that you came from another sphere than this absurd world, where, with the best inclinations, I cannot open my ears. I am a wretched creature, and yet I complain of others!! You will forgive this from the goodness of heart that beams in your eyes, and the good sense manifested by your ears;—at least they understand how to flatter, by the mode in which they listen. My ears are, alas! a partition-wall, through which I can with difficulty hold any intercourse with my fellow-creatures. Otherwise, perhaps, I might have felt more assured with you; but I was only conscious of the full, intelligent glance from your eyes, which affected me so deeply that never can I forget it. My dear friend! dearest girl!—Art! who comprehends it? with whom can I discuss this mighty goddess? How precious to me were the few days when we talked together, or, I should rather say, corresponded! I have carefully preserved the little notes with your clever, charming, most charming answers, so I have to thank my defective hearing for the greater part of our fugitive intercourse being written down. Since you left this I have had some unhappy hours—hours of the deepest gloom, when I could do nothing. I wandered for three hours in the Schönbrunn Allée after you left us, but no *angel* met me there to take possession of me as you did. Pray forgive, my dear friend, this deviation from the original key, but I must have such intervals as a relief to my heart. You have no doubt written to Goethe about me? I would gladly bury my head in a sack, so that I might neither see nor hear what goes on in the world, because I shall meet you there no more; but I shall get a letter from you? Hope sustains me, as it does half the world; through life she has been my close companion, or what would have become of me? I send you 'Kennst Du das Land,' written with my own hand, as a remembrance of the hour when I first knew you; I send you also another that I composed since I bade you farewell, my dearest, fairest sweet-heart!

> Herz, mein Herz, was soll das geben,
> Was bedränget dich so sehr;
> Welch ein neues fremdes Leben,
> Ich erkenne dich nicht mehr.

Now answer me, my dearest friend, and say what is to become of me since my heart has turned such a rebel. Write to your most faithful friend,

BEETHOVEN

67.

*To Bettina Brentano.*

Vienna, Feb. 10, 1811.

Dear and beloved Friend,

I have now received two letters from you, while those to Tonie show that you still remember me, and even too kindly. I carried your letter about with me the whole summer, and it often made me feel very happy: though I do not frequently write to you, and you never see me, still I write you letters by thousands in my thoughts. I can easily imagine what you feel at Berlin in witnessing all the noxious frivolity of the world's rabble,* even had you not written it to me yourself. Such prating about art, and yet no results!!! The best description of this is to be found in Schiller's poem 'Die Flüsse,' where the river Spree is supposed to speak. You are going to be married, my dear friend, or are already so, and I have had no chance of seeing you even once previously. May all the felicity that marriage ever bestowed on husband and wife attend you both! What can I say to you of myself? I can only exclaim with Johanna, 'Compassionate my fate!' If I am spared for some years to come, I will thank the Omniscient, the Omnipotent, for the boon, as I do for all other weal and woe. If you mention me when you write to Goethe,

---

* An expression which, as well as many others, he no doubt borrowed from Bettina, and introduced to please her.

strive to find words expressive of my deep reverence and admiration. I am about to write to him myself with regard to 'Egmont,' for which I have written some music solely from my love for his poetry, which always delights me. Who can be sufficiently grateful to a great poet—the most precious jewel of a nation! Now no more, my dear sweet friend! I only came home this morning at four o'clock from an orgy, where I laughed heartily, but to-day I feel as if I could weep as sadly: turbulent pleasures always violently recoil on my spirits. As for Clemens [Brentano, her brother], pray thank him for his complaisance; with regard to the Cantata, the subject is not important enough for us here—it is very different in Berlin; and as for my affection, the sister engrosses so large a share, that little remains for the brother. Will he be content with this?

Now farewell, my dear, dear friend; I imprint a sorrowful kiss on your forehead, thus impressing my thoughts on it as with a seal. Write soon, very soon, to your brother,

BEETHOVEN.

68.

*To Zmeskall.*

1811.

I am disposed to engage a man who has just offered me his services—a music-copyist; his parents live in Vienna, which might be convenient in many respects, but I first wish to speak to you about the terms, and as you

are disengaged to-morrow, which I, *alas*! am every day,
I beg you will take coffee with me in the afternoon,
when we can discuss the matter, and then proceed from
*words to deeds*. We have also the honour to inform
you that we intend shortly to confer on you some of
the decorations of the Order of our Household—the first
class for yourself, the others for anyone you choose—
except a priest. We shall expect your answer early
to-morrow. We now present you with some blotches
of ink.

Your BEETHOVEN.

### 69.

### *To Zmeskall.*

1811.

Most high-born of men !

We beg you to confer some goose-quills on us; we
will in return send you a whole bunch of the same
sort, that you may not be obliged to pluck out your own.
It is just possible that you may yet receive the Grand
Cross of the Order of the Violoncello. We remain
your gracious and most friendly of all friends,

BEETHOVEN.

### 70.

### *To the Archduke Rudolph.**

The Spring of 1811.

Your Royal Highness,

As in spite of every effort I can find no copyist to
write in my house, I send you my own manuscript : all

---

\* Schlemmer was for many years Beethoven's copyist.

you have to do is to desire Schlemmer to get you an efficient copyist, who must, however, write out the Trio in your palace, otherwise there would be no security against piracy.  I am better, and hope to have the honour of waiting on you in the course of a few days, when we must strive to make up for lost time.  I always feel anxious and uneasy when I do not attend Your Royal Highness as often or as assiduously as I wish. It is certainly the truth when I say that the loss is mine, but I trust I shall not soon again be so unwell.    Be graciously pleased to remember me; the time may yet come when I shall be able to show you doubly and trebly that I deserve this more than ever.

I am Your Royal Highness's devoted servant,

LUDWIG V. BEETHOVEN.


### 71.

My dear Friend,*

I have taken this trouble only that I might figure correctly, and thus be able sometimes to lead others. As for mistakes, I scarcely ever required to have them pointed out to me, having had from my childhood such

* Written on a sheet of music-paper (oblong folio) numbered 22, and evidently torn out of a large book.  On the other side (21) is written, in Beethoven's hand, instructions on the use of the fourth in retardations, with five musical examples.  The leaf is no doubt torn from one of the books that Beethoven had compiled from various text-books, for the instruction of the Archduke Rudolph.  I have therefore placed Beethoven's remark here.

a quick perception, that I exercised it unconscious that it ought to be so, or in fact could be otherwise.

### 72.

#### To the dramatic Poet Treitschke.

June 6, 1811.

Dear Treitschke,

Have you read the book, and may I venture to hope that you will be persuaded to undertake it? Be so good as to give me an answer, as I am prevented going to you myself. If you have already read it, then send it back to me, that I may also look over it again before you begin to work at it. Above all, if it be your good pleasure that I should soar to the skies on the wings of your poetry, I entreat you to effect this as soon as possible.

Your obedient servant,

L. v. BEETHOVEN.

### 73.

#### To Zmeskall.

Sept. 10, 1811.

Dear Zmeskall,

Let the rehearsal stand over for the present. I must see my doctor again to-day, of whose bungling I begin to tire. Thanks for your metronome; let us try whether we can measure Time into Eternity with it, for it is so *simple* and *easily managed* that there seems to be no impediment to this! In the meantime we will have a conference on the subject. The mathematical precision of clockwork is of course greater, yet formerly, in watching the little experiments you made in my presence, I thought there was something worthy of notice in your metronome, and I hope we shall soon succeed in *setting it thoroughly right.* Ere long I hope to see you.

Your friend,

BEETHOVEN.

## 74.

### *To Zmeskall.*

Oct. 26, 1811.

I shall be at the 'Swan' to-day, and hope to meet you there *to a certainty,* but don't come too late. My foot is better; the author of so many poetical *feet* promises the *head* author a sound foot within a week's time.

## 75.

### *To Zmeskall.*

Nov. 20, 1811.

We are deucedly obliged to you. We beg you to be careful not to lose your well-earned fame. You are exhorted to pursue the same course, and we remain once more your deucedly attached

LUDWIG VAN BEETHOVEN.

### 76.

*To Zmeskall.*

I shall be at the 'Swan' to-day, dear Z. I have, alas! *too much* leisure, and you *none*!

Your BEETHOVEN.

### 77.

*To Zmeskall.**

1812.

Confounded little quondam musical Count!

What the deuce has become of you? Are you to be at the 'Swan' to-day? No? . . . Yes! See from this enclosure what I have done for Hungary. When a German undertakes a thing, even without pledging his word, he acts very differently from one of those Hungarian Counts, such as B. [Brunswick], who allowed me to travel by myself—from what paltry, miserable motive who can tell?—and kept me waiting, though he did not wait for me!

My excellent little quondam musical Count,

I am now, as ever, your attached

BEETHÖVERL.

Return the enclosure, for we wish to bring it, and something else, pretty forcibly under the notice of the Count.

---

* The date of this and the following note is decided by the allusion to his compositions written for Hungary (Pesth). See the subsequent letter to Varenna.

78.

*To Zmeskall.*

You are summoned to appear to-day at the ' Swan ; '
Brunswick also comes. If you do not appear, you are
henceforth excluded from all that concerns us. Excuses
*per excellentiam* cannot be accepted. Obedience is
enjoined, knowing that we are acting for your benefit,
and that our motive is to guard you against temptations
and faithlessness *per excellentiam—dixi.*

BEETHOVEN.

79.

*To Zmeskall.*

Dear Zmeskall,

The well-known watchmaker who lives close to the
Freiung is to call on you. I want a first-rate repeater,
for which he asks forty ducats. As you like that kind
of thing, I beg you will exert yourself on my behalf,
and select a really good watch for me.

With the most enthusiastic admiration for a man like
yourself, who is soon to give me an opportunity of
displaying in his favour my particular knowledge of
horn-playing,

I am your

LUDWIG VAN BEETHOVEN.

80.

*To Kammerprocurator Varenna,—Gratz.**

1812.

If the wish to benefit the poor were not so evident in your letter, I should have felt not a little offended by your accompanying your request to me by the offer of payment. From my childhood, whenever my art could be serviceable to poor suffering humanity, I have never allowed any other motive to influence me, and never required anything beyond the heartfelt gratification that it always caused me. With this you will receive an Oratorio — (A), the performance of which occupies half an evening, also an Overture and a Fantasia with Chorus—(B). If in your benevolent Institution you possess a *dépôt* for such things, I beg you will deposit these three works there, as a mark of my sympathy for the destitute ; to be considered as their property, and to be given at any concerts intended for

* The correspondence with Varenna, consisting of fourteen letters and four notes, was purchased some years ago by a collector of autographs in Leipzig, and sold again by public auction, probably to different persons. It would be like pursuing leaves scattered by the wind to try to recover these letters. Those here given have for the most part appeared in newspapers; I cannot, therefore, be responsible for the text, further than their publication goes, which, however, has evidently been conducted by a clever hand. The date of the first letter is to be gleaned from the second, and we also learn from them that 'The Ruins of Athens' and King Stephen' (or at all events the Overture) were already finished in January 1812.

their sole benefit. In addition to these, you will receive an Introduction to the ' Ruins of Athens,' the score of which shall be written out for you as soon as possible. Likewise a Grand Overture to ' Ungarn's erste Wohl-thäter ' [Hungary's First Benefactors].

Both form part of two works that I wrote for the Hungarians at the opening of their new theatre [in Pesth]. Pray give me, however, your written assurance that these works shall not be performed elsewhere, as they are not published, nor likely to be so for some time to come. You shall receive the latter Grand Overture as soon as it is returned to me from Hungary, which it will be in the course of a few days.

The engraved Fantasia with Chorus could no doubt be executed by a lady, an amateur, mentioned to me here by Professor Schneller.* The words after the Chorus No. 4, in C major, were altered by the publishers, and are now quite contrary to the musical expression ; those written in *pencil*, therefore, on the music must be

* This dilettante was Mdlle. Marie Koschak, subsequently the wife of Dr. Pachler, an advocate in Gratz, from whom two letters are given by Schindler of the dates of August 15th, 1825, and November 5th, 1826, in which she invites Beethoven to visit her in Gratz. Schindler considers as applicable to this lady the words of a note in Beethoven's writing of which he has given a facsimile in his ' Biography,' i. 95 ; the date 1817 or 1818. They are as follows :—' Love alone, yes ! love alone can make your life happier. Oh, God ! grant that I may at last find her who can strengthen me in virtue, whom I can legitimately call my own. On July 27th, when she drove past me in Baden, she seemed to gaze at me.' This lady also plays a friendly part in Franz Schubert's ' Life.' See her ' Biography ' by Dr. Kreissle.

sung. If you can make use of the Oratorio, I can send you *all the parts written out,* so that the outlay may be less for the poor. Write to me about this.

Your obedient

LUDWIG VAN BEETHOVEN.

81.

*To Zmeskall.*

Feb. 2, 1812.

By no means *extraordinary,* but *very ordinary* mender of pens! whose talent has failed on this occasion (for those I send require to be fresh mended), when do you intend at last to cast off your fetters?— when? You never for a moment think of me: accursed to me is life amid this Austrian barbarism. I shall go now chiefly to the ' Swan,' as in other taverns I cannot defend myself against intrusion. Farewell! that is, *fare as well* as I wish you to do without

Your friend,

BEETHOVEN.

Most wonderful of men! We beg that your servant will engage a person to fit up my apartment; as he is acquainted with the lodgings, he can fix the proper price at once. Do this soon, you Carnival scamp!!!!!!!

The enclosed note is at least a week old.

## 82.

### To Zmeskall.

Feb. 8, 1812.

Most extraordinary and first and foremost man of the pendulum in the world, and without a lever too ! ! !

I am much indebted to you for having imparted to me some share of your motive power. I wish to express my gratitude in person, and therefore invite you this morning to come to the ' Swan ;' a tavern, the name of which itself shows that it is a fitting place when such a subject is in question.

Yours ever,

BEETHOVEN.

## 83.

### To Varenna,—Gratz.

Vienna, Feb. 8, 1812.

Herr Rettich has already got the parts of the Oratorio, and when you no longer require them I beg you will send them back to me. It is not probable that anything is wanting, but even in that case, as you have the score, you can easily remedy this. I only yesterday received the Overtures from Hungary, and shall have them copied and forwarded to you as soon as possible. I likewise send a March with a vocal Chorus, also from the ' Ruins of Athens.' Altogether you will now have sufficient to fill up the time.

As these pieces are only in manuscript, I shall let

you know at the time I send them what precautions I
wish you to take with regard to the Overtures and the
March with Chorus.

As I do not publish any new work until a year after
its composition, and, when I do so, am obliged invariably
to give a written assurance to the publisher that no one
is in possession of it, you can yourself perceive that I
must carefully guard against any possible contingency
or casualty as to these pieces.   I must, however, assure
you that I shall always be disposed to show the warmest
zeal in aid of your charity, and I here pledge myself to
send you every year works that exist solely in manuscript, or compositions written expressly for this charitable purpose.   I beg you will also let me know what
your future plans are with regard to your Institution,
that I may act accordingly.

Farewell !   I remain, with the highest consideration,
                    Your obedient
                         LUDWIG VAN BEETHOVEN.

### 84.

### *To Zmeskall.**

Feb. 19, 1812.

Dear Z.,

I only yesterday received the written information
that the Archduke pays his share in the new paper-

* The Finance Patent appeared in Austria in 1811, by which the
value of money was depreciated by a fifth.   This also affected the salary
that Beethoven drew from the Archduke Rudolph, Prince Kinsky, and
Prince Lobkowitz.   The first of these gentlemen paid his full share in

money of the full value [*Einlösungsschein*]. I beg you will write out for me, as nearly as you can, the substance of what you said on Sunday, and which we thought it advisable to send to the other two. I am offered a certificate that the Archduke is to pay in *Einlösungsschein*, but I think this unnecessary, more especially as the people about Court, in spite of all their apparent friendship for me, declare that my demands are *not just*!!!! Oh, Heaven! aid me in enduring this! I am no Hercules, to help Atlas in carrying the world, or to strive to do so in his place. It was only yesterday that I heard the particulars of the handsome manner in which Baron von Kraft had judged and spoken of me to Zisius! But never mind, dear Z.! My endurance of these shameful attacks cannot continue much longer; persecuted art will everywhere find an asylum—Dædalus, though imprisoned in a labyrinth, found wings to carry him aloft. Oh! I too shall find wings!

Yours ever,

BEETHOVEN.

If you have time, send me this morning the draft of the memorial;—probably for nothing, and to receive nothing! so much time is already lost, and only to be kept in suspense by civil words!

*Einlösungsschein.* Lobkowitz, at the request of Beethoven, soon after did the same; with Kinsky's share alone difficulties arose subsequently, owing to his death.

85.

*To Varenna.*

In spite of my anxiety to serve the cause of your charity, I have been quite unable to do so. I have no copyist of my own to write for me as formerly, and the limited time renders it impossible for me to do so myself, thus I am obliged to have recourse to strangers as copyists. One of these promised to write out the Overtures, &c. &c., for you ; but Passion Week intervening, when there are so many concerts, prevented his being able to keep his word, in spite of every effort on my part. Even if the Overtures and the March with Chorus were transcribed, it would not be possible to send them by this post, and if we wait for the next, the music will arrive too late for Easter Sunday. Let me know if there are any means you could adopt to gain a little more time, or any chance opportunity of sending these works to you, and I will do all that lies in my power to aid the cause of your charity.

I am, with esteem, yours obediently,

LUDWIG VAN BEETHOVEN.

## 86.

### *To the Archduke Rudolph.*\*

1812.

Your Imperial Highness,

I was much vexed not to receive Y. I. H.'s message to come to you till very late yesterday evening—indeed nearly at eleven o'clock. Contrary to my usual custom, I did not go home at all during the afternoon, the fine weather having tempted me to spend the whole afternoon in walking, and the evening at the Banda, 'auf der Wieden,' and thus I was not aware of your wish till I returned home. In the meantime, whenever Y. I. H. desires it, I am ready at any hour or moment to place myself at your disposal. I therefore await your gracious commands.

I am Your Imperial Highness's most obedient

LUDWIG VAN BEETHOVEN.

## 87.

### *To the Archduke Rudolph.*

1812.

Your Imperial Highness,

I was unable till to-day, when I leave my bed for the first time, to answer your gracious letter. It will be impossible for me to wait on you to-morrow, but perhaps the day after. I have suffered much

---

\* The date 1812 is marked on the sheet by another hand, and the close of the second note proves that it was at the commencement of this year.

during the last few days, and I may 'say twofold from
not being in a condition to devote a great part of
my time to you, according to my heartfelt wish.    I
hope now, however, to have cleared off all scores for
spring and summer (I mean as to health).

I am Your Imperial Highness's most obdt. servant,

LUDWIG VAN BEETHOVEN.

### 88.

*To Varenna,—Gratz.*

Vienna, May 8, 1812.

Sir,

Being still far from well, and much occupied, I have
been unable to reply to your letters.    How in the world
did such an unfounded idea ever occur to you as that I
was displeased ?    It would certainly have been better
had you returned the music as soon as it had been performed, for at that period I could have produced it
here, whereas now, unluckily, it comes too late ; but I
only say *unluckily* because it prevents my being able
to spare the worthy ladies the expenses of copying.    At
any other time I would on no account have allowed
them to pay for writing out the works, but it so happens
that at this moment I am visited with every kind of
*contretemps,* so I cannot avoid doing so.    Possibly
Herr O., although with the best intentions, has delayed informing you of this, which obliged me to apply to him for repayment of the expenses of copying

—perhaps, too, in my haste, I did not express myself
distinctly. You can now, esteemed Sir, have the Overture and the Chorus again if you require them.

I feel convinced that in any event you will prevent
my confidence being abused ; in the meantime you may
keep the Overture on the conditions I have stated. If I
find that I am able to pay for the copying, I will re-
deem it for my own use.

The score of the Oratorio is a gift, and also the
Overture to 'Egmont.' Keep the parts of the Oratorio
beside you till you can have it performed.

Select whatever you choose for the concert which I
hear you now intend to give, and if you decide on the
Chorus and the Overture, they shall be forwarded to
you at once. For the future concert, for the benefit of
the venerable Ursulines, I promise you an entirely new
Symphony at all events, and perhaps also a work of
some importance for voices, and as I have now a favourable opportunity, the copying shall not cost you a
farthing. My joy would be beyond all bounds if the
concert were to be successful, and I could spare you all
expense ;—at all events, take my good will for granted.

Remember me to the admirable teachers of the children, and say to them that I shed tears of joy at the
happy result of my poor good will, and that so far as
my humble capabilities can serve them, they shall always find in me the warmest sympathy.

My cordial thanks for your invitation ; I would fain

become acquainted with the interesting scenery of Styria, and possibly I may one day enjoy that pleasure. Farewell! I heartily rejoice in having found in you a friend to the poor and needy, and am always yours to command.

LUDWIG VAN BEETHOVEN, M.P.

89.

*To Joseph Freiherr von Schweiger, Chamberlain of the Archduke Rudolph.*

1812.

The most insignificant of mortals has just been to wait on his gracious master, when he found everything closed, so he came here, where indeed all was *open*, but no one to be found except the trusty servant. I had a heavy packet of music with me, in order to ensure a good musical evening before we parted; but in vain. Malfatti † is resolved that I shall go to Töplitz, which is anything but agreeable to me. As, however, I must obey, I hope at least that my gracious master will not enjoy himself quite so much without me. *O vanitas!* for it is nothing else. Before I set off for Töplitz I will either go to Baden to see you or write. Farewell! Pray present my homage to my gracious master, and continue your regard for

Your friend,

[K.]                                    BEETHOVEN.

* The journey to Töplitz took place in the year 1812.

† A very celebrated physician in Vienna at that time, consulted by Beethoven.

### 90.

*To Varenna,—Gratz.*

Töplitz, July 19, 1812.

My thanks have been too long delayed for all the dainties which the worthy ladies sent for my enjoyment; being constantly ill in Vienna, I was at last forced to take refuge here.

However, better late than never, so I beg you will say all sorts of kind things in my name to the admirable Ursuline ladies, though I did not deserve so much gratitude; indeed it is rather for me to thank Him who enables me to render my art occasionally useful to others. When you next wish to make use of my poor abilities for the benefit of the venerable ladies, you have only to write to me.

A new Symphony is now ready for you, and as the Archduke Rudolph has had it copied out, it will cost you nothing. Perhaps I may one of these days be able to send you something vocal. I only wish and hope that you will not ascribe my anxiety to serve these venerable ladies to a certain degree of vanity or desire for fame, as this would grieve me exceedingly. If these good ladies wish to do me any service in return, I beg they will include me with their pupils in their pious orisons. I remain, with esteem,

Your friend,

LUDWIG VAN BEETHOVEN.

I shall remain here for some weeks, so if there is any occasion to write, address to me here.

## 91.

*Written in the Album of the Singer, Mdme. Auguste Sebald.*

Töplitz, August 8, 1812.

LUDWIG VAN BEETHOVEN,

Who even if you would,
Forget you never should.

## 92.

*To H. R. Highness the Archduke Rudolph.*

Franzensbrunn, Aug. 12, 1812.

It was my bounden duty long ago to have recalled myself to Y. R. H.'s recollection, but partly my occupations and the state of my health, as well as my own insignificance, made me reluctant to do so. I missed Y. R. H. by one night only in Prague; for when proceeding to pay my respects to you in the morning, I found you had set off the very night before. In Töplitz I heard a military band four times a day—the only musical report which I can give you. I was a great deal with Goethe.* My physician Staudenheim,† however,

---

* Beethoven speaks very briefly of his meeting with Goethe. Goethe in his 'Tag- und Jahrschriften' of 1812 makes no allusion to Beethoven during his stay at Töplitz. It does not, therefore, appear that either of these master minds found any particular pleasure in each other when they met personally. Beethoven, indeed, dedicated to 'the immortal Goethe' (1812) his composition the 'Meeresstille und glückliche Fahrt,' but only wrote once to him in 1823 to obtain a subscription from the Grand Duke of Weimar for his Grand Mass, and received no answer from Goethe. In the complete edition of Goethe's works Beethoven's name is only once mentioned by Goethe, when he refers to his funeral obsequies.

† Dr. Staudenheim was, like Malfatti, one of the most celebrated phy-

ordered me off to Carlsbad, and from thence here, and probably I shall have to go back to Töplitz from this. What flights! And yet it seems very doubtful whether any improvement in my condition has hitherto taken place. I receive the best accounts of Y. R. H.'s health, and also of the persistent devotion you exhibit towards the musical Muse. Y. R. H. has no doubt heard of a concert that I gave for the benefit of the sufferers by fire in the Stadt Baden,* assisted by Herr Polledro.† The receipts were nearly 1,000 florins W. W., and if I had not been restricted in my arrangements we might easily have taken 2,000 florins. It was literally a *poor concert for the poor.* I could only find at the publisher's here some of my earlier Sonatas with violin accompaniments, and as Polledro had set his heart on these, I was obliged to content myself with playing an old Sonata.‡ The entire concert consisted of a Trio, in which Polledro played, my Sonata with violin, then again something was played by Polledro, and, lastly, I extemporised.

sicians in Vienna. Beethoven, too, was well acquainted with Staudenheim, but in his regimen he neither followed the prescriptions of Staudenheim nor of Malfatti.

* The Stadt Baden, near Vienna, had been visited on July 16th by a most destructive conflagration.

† Giov. Batt. Polledro, Kapellmeister in Turin, born 1776, travelled through Germany as a violinist from 1809 to 1812. He gave a concert in Vienna in March 1812.

‡ The violin Sonata with pianoforte was probably Op. 47 (composed in 1803 and published in 1805, according to Thayer, No. 111), or one of his earlier compositions, Op. 30, or 24, or 23.

Meanwhile I do sincerely rejoice that by this means something has fallen to the share of the poor *Badeners.* Pray deign to accept my best wishes for your welfare, and my entreaty that you will sometimes think of me.

[K.]

93.

*To Bettina von Arnim.*

Töplitz, August 15, 1812.

My most dear kind Friend,

Kings and princes can indeed create professors and privy-counsellors, and confer titles and decorations, but they cannot make great men—spirits that soar above the base turmoil of this world. There their powers fail, and this it is that forces them to respect us.* When two persons like Goethe and myself meet, these grandees cannot fail to perceive what such as we consider great. Yesterday, on our way home, we met the whole Imperial family; we saw them coming some way off, when Goethe withdrew his arm from mine, in order to stand aside, and say what I would, I could not prevail on him to make another step in advance. I pressed down my hat more firmly on my head, buttoned up my great coat, and, crossing my arms behind me, I made my way through the thickest portion of the crowd. Princes and cour-

---

* Fräulein Giannatasio del Rio, in the journal she sent to the ' Grenz Boten ' in 1857, states that Beethoven once declared, ' It is very pleasant to associate with the great of the earth, but one must possess some quality which inspires them with respect.'

tiers formed a lane for me; Archduke Rudolph took off his hat, and the Empress bowed to me first. These great ones of the earth *know me*. To my infinite amusement, I saw the procession defile past Goethe, who stood aside with his hat off, bowing profoundly. I afterwards took him sharply to task for this; I gave him no quarter, and upbraided him with all his sins, especially towards you, my dear friend, as we had just been speaking of you. Heavens! if I could have lived with you as *he* did, believe me I should have produced far greater things. A musician is also a poet, he too can feel himself transported into a brighter world by a pair of fine eyes, where loftier spirits sport with him and impose heavy tasks on him. What thoughts rushed into my mind when I first saw you in the Observatory during a refreshing May shower, so fertilising to me also!\* The most beautiful themes stole from your eyes into my heart, which shall yet enchant the world when Beethoven no longer *directs*. If God vouchsafes to grant me a few more years of life, I must then see you once more, my dear, most dear friend, for the voice within, to which I always listen, demands this. Spirits may love one another, and I shall ever woo yours. Your approval is dearer to me than all else in the world. I told Goethe my sentiments as to the influence praise has over men like us, and that we desire our equals to listen to us

---

\* According to Bettina (see ' Goethe's Correspondence with a Child,' ii. 193), their first acquaintance was made in Beethoven's apartments.

with their understanding. Emotion suits women only; (forgive me !) music ought to strike fire from the soul of a man. Ah ! my dear girl, how long have our feelings been identical on all points ! ! ! The sole real good is some bright kindly spirit to sympathise with us, whom we thoroughly comprehend, and from whom we need not hide our thoughts. *He who wishes to appear something, must in reality be something.* The world must acknowledge us, it is not always unjust; but for this I care not, having a higher purpose in view. I hope to get a letter from you in Vienna; write to me soon and fully, for a week hence I shall be there. The Court leaves this to-morrow, and to-day they have another performance. The Empress has studied her part thoroughly. The Emperor and the Duke wished me to play some of my own music, but I refused, for they are both infatuated with *Chinese porcelain.* A little indulgence is required, for reason seems to have lost its empire ; but I do not choose to minister to such perverse folly—I will not be a party to such absurd doings to please those Princes who are constantly guilty of eccentricities of this sort. Adieu ! adieu ! dear one ; your letter lay all night next my heart, and cheered me. Musicians permit themselves great licence. *Heavens ! how I love you !* Your most faithful friend and deaf brother,

BEETHOVEN.

## 94.

*To Princess Kinsky,—Prague.*

Vienna, Dec. 30, 1812.

Your Highness,

The dreadful event which deprived you of your husband, Prince von Kinsky, snatching him from his fatherland and from all those who love him,* as well as from many whom he generously supported, filling every heart capable of, appreciating goodness and greatness with the deepest sorrow, affected me also in the most profound and painful degree. The stern duty of self-interest compels me to lay before Your Highness a humble petition, the reasonable purport of which may, I hope, plead my excuse for intruding on Your Highness at a time when so many affairs of importance claim your attention. Permit me to state the matter to Your Highness.

Y. H. is no doubt aware that when I received a summons to Westphalia in the year 1809, His Highness Prince von Kinsky, your late husband, together with His I. H. Archduke Rudolph and H. H. the Prince von Lobkowitz, offered to settle on me for life an annual income of 4,000 gulden, provided I declined the proposal in question, and determined to remain in Austria. Although this sum was by no means in proportion to

---

* Prince Josef Ferdinand Kinsky, born December 1781, and killed by a fall from his horse, November 3, 1812.

that secured to me in Westphalia, still my predilection for Austria, as well as my sense of this most generous proposal, induced me to accept it without hesitation. The share contributed by H. H. Prince Kinsky consisted of 1,800 florins, which I have received by quarterly instalments since 1809 from the Prince's privy purse. Though subsequent occurrences partially diminished this sum, I rested satisfied, till the appearance of the Finance Patent, reducing bank notes into *Einlösung Schein*. I applied to H. I. H. the Archduke Rudolph to request that the portion of the annuity contributed by H. I. H. should in future be paid in *Einlösung Schein*. This was at once granted, and I received a written assurance to that effect from H. I. H. Prince von Lobkowitz agreed to the same with regard to his share—700 florins [see No. 84]. H. H. Prince von Kinsky being at that time in Prague, I addressed my respectful petition to him last May, through Herr Varnhagen von Ense, an officer in the Vogelsang Regiment, that His Highness's contribution to my salary —1,800 florins—should be paid like the rest in *Einlösung Schein*. Herr von Varnhagen wrote as follows, and the original of the letter is still extant :—

' I had yesterday the desired interview with Prince Kinsky. With the highest praise of Beethoven, he at once acceded to his demand, and is prepared to pay up the arrears, and also all future sums from the date of the *Einlösung Schein*, in that currency. The cashier here has received the necessary instructions, and Beethoven can draw for the whole sum on his way through Prague, or, if he prefers it, in Vienna, as soon as the Prince returns there.

'Prague : June 9th, 1812.'

When passing through Prague some weeks afterwards, I took the opportunity of waiting on the Prince, and received from him the fullest confirmation of this promise. H. H. likewise assured me that he entirely admitted the propriety of my demand, and considered it quite reasonable.  As I could not remain in Prague till this affair was finally settled, H. H. was so kind as to make me a payment of sixty ducats on account, which, ac cording to H. H.'s calculation, were good for 600 florins, Vienna currency.  The arrears were to be paid up on my return to Vienna, and an order giver to the cashier to pay my salary in future in *Einlösung Schein.* Such was H. H.'s pleasure.  My illness increasing in Töplitz, I was obliged to remain there longer than I originally intended.  In the month of September I therefore addressed to H. H., who was then in Vienna, through one of my friends here, Herr Oliva, a written memorial, claiming his promise, when H. H. graciously repeated to this friend the assurance he had already given me, adding that in the course of a few days he would give the necessary instructions on the subject to his cashier.

A short time afterwards he left Vienna.  When I

arrived there, I enquired from the Prince's secretary whether H. H. had given directions about my salary before leaving Vienna, when, to my surprise, I was told that H. H. had done nothing in the matter.

My title to the liquidation of my claim is proved by the testimony of the Herren von Varnhagen and Oliva, to whom H. H. spoke on the subject, reiterating his consent. I feel convinced that the illustrious heirs and family of this Prince will in the same spirit of benevolence and generosity strive to fulfil his intentions. I therefore confidently place in Y. H.'s hands my respectful petition, viz., ' to pay up the arrears of my salary in *Einlösung Schein,* and to instruct your cashier to transmit me the amount in future, in the same currency.' Relying on your sense of justice according me a favourable decision, I remain Y. H.'s

Most obedient servant,

LUDWIG VAN BEETHOVEN.

95.

*To the Archduke Rudolph.*

1813.*

I have been far from well since last Sunday, but have suffered more in mind than in body. I beg your forgiveness a thousand times for not having sooner sent my apologies; each day I had the strongest inclination to wait on you, but Heaven knows that in spite of the

---

* Prince Franz Josef Lobkowitz died December 25th, 1816. His musical meetings were certainly continued till 1813, or longer.

best will that I always entertain for the best of masters
I was unable to do so, distressing as it is to me not to
have it in my power to sacrifice all to him for whom
I cherish the highest esteem, love, and veneration.
Y. R. H. would perhaps act wisely in making a pause
at present with the Lobkowitz concerts : even the most
brilliant talent may lose its effect by too great fami-
liarity.

[K.]

## 96.

### To the Archduke Rudolph.

1813.*

At early dawn to-morrow the copyist shall begin the
last movement. As I am in the meantime writing several
other works, I did not hurry myself much with this last
movement merely for the sake of punctuality, especially
as I must write this more deliberately, with a view to
Rode's† playing: we like quick, full-toned passages in our

---

* 1813.   January—February.

† Pierre Rode, the violinist, arrived in Vienna in January 1813, and
gave a concert in the Redoutensaal on February 6th, but did not give
universal satisfaction ('A. M. Z.,' 1813, p. 114), and a second concert that
he had projected does not appear to have taken place.   He played in
Gratz on February 20th and 27th.   It seems that Rode was to play with
Beethoven at the Archduke Rudolph's, for which occasion Beethoven prepared a composition for them both.   Was this the Sonata for pianoforte
and violin, Op. 36, which he afterwards dedicated to the Archduke?
Thayer states that it was written by Beethoven in 1810, and sold to the
music publisher Steiner in Vienna in April 1815.   No other composition
for the violin and pianoforte is so likely to be the one as this.   It is, how-

Finales, which do not suit R., and this rather cramps
me.  At all events, all is sure to go well next Tuesday.
I very much doubt whether I shall be able to present
myself at Y. R. H.'s on that evening, in spite of my
zeal in your service; but to make up for this, I mean to
come to you to-morrow forenoon and to-morrow afternoon, that I may entirely fulfil the wishes of my illustrious pupil.

[K.]

## 97.

### To the Archduke Rudolph.

1813.

I had just gone out yesterday when your gracious
letter reached me.  As for my health, it is pretty much
the same, particularly as moral causes affect it, which
do not seem likely to be removed ; particularly as I
can have recourse to no one but myself for aid, and can
find help in my own head alone ; and more particularly
still, because in these days neither words, nor honour,
nor written pledges, seem binding on anyone.  As for
my occupations, I have come to an end with some of
them, and, even without your gracious invitation, I intended to appear at the usual hour to-day.  With re-

ever, a mistake in the 'Bibliothèque Universelle,' tome xxxvi. p. 210, to
state that Beethoven during Rode's stay in Vienna composed the ' déli-
cieuse Romance ' which was played with so much expression by De Baillot
on the violin.  There are only two Romances known for the violin by
Beethoven, the one in G major, Op. 40, in the year 1803, and the second
in F major, Op. 50, published in 1805.  (Thayer, 102 and 104.)

gard to Rode [See No. 96], I beg Y. R. H. to be so good
as to let me have the part by the bearer of this, and I
will send it to him at once, with a polite note from me.
*He certainly will not take amiss my sending him the
part. Oh! certainly not! Would to Heaven that I
were obliged to ask his forgiveness on this account! for
in that case things would really be in a better position.* Is it your pleasure that I should come to you this
evening at five o'clock as usual, or does Y. R. H. desire another hour? I shall endeavour to arrange accordingly, and punctually to fulfil your wishes.

[K.]

## 98.

### To Princess Kinsky.

Vienna, Feb. 12, 1813.

Your Highness!

You were so gracious as to declare with regard to
the salary settled on me by your deceased husband,
that you saw the propriety of my receiving it in
Vienna currency, but that the authority of the court of
law which has assumed the guardianship of the estate
must first be obtained. Under the conviction that the
authorities who represent their princely wards could not
fail to be influenced by the same motives that actuated
the late Prince in his conduct towards me, I think I
am justified in expecting the ratification of my claim
from the aforesaid court, as I can prove, by the testimony of well-known, respectable, and upright men the

promise and intentions of H. H. in my behalf, which cannot fail to be binding on his heirs and children. If, therefore, the proofs submitted should even be found deficient in legal formality, I cannot doubt that this want will be supplied by the noble mode of thinking of this illustrious house, and by their own inclination to generous actions.

Possibly another question may at present arise from the condition of the inheritance, which is no doubt heavily burdened, both owing to the melancholy and sudden death of the late Prince, and by the state of the times, which renders it equally just and indispensable to husband carefully all possible resources. On this account it is far from my wish to claim more than is absolutely necessary for my own livelihood, and grounded on the contract itself—the legality of such a claim on the heirs of the late Prince not being in any way disputed.

I beg, then, that Y. H. will be pleased to direct the arrears of my salary, due since the 1st September, 1811, calculated in Vienna currency, in accordance with the scale of the contract making in W.W. 1,088 florins 42 kreuzers, to be paid, and *in the interim*, the question whether this salary ought to be paid in Vienna currency can be deferred until the affairs are settled, when the subject is again brought before the trustees, and my claims admitted to be just by their consent and authority. The late Prince having given me sixty ducats

merely on account of my salary, which was to be paid
by agreement in Vienna currency, and as this agreement (as every intelligent man will inform Y. H.) must
be accepted to its full extent, or at all events not cause
me loss, it follows as a matter of course that Y. H. will
not object to my considering the sixty ducats as only an
instalment of the arrears due to me beyond the usual
scale of payment, agreed to be paid in Vienna currency,
so that the amount must not be deducted from the sum
still due to me.

I feel sure that Y. H.'s noble feelings will do justice
to the equity of my proposal, and my wish to enter into
every detail of this affair, so far as circumstances permit, and also my readiness to postpone my claims to
suit your convenience. The same elevated sentiments
which prompted you to fulfil the engagement entered
into by the late Prince, will also make Y. H. apprehend
the absolute necessity entailed on me by my position
again to solicit immediate payment of the arrears of my
salary, which are indispensable for my maintenance.

Anxiously hoping for a favourable answer to my
petition, I have the honour to remain, with profound
respect,

Y. R. H.'s obedient servant,

LUDWIG VAN BEETHOVEN.

## 99.

### *To Princess Kinsky.*

Highly honoured Princess!

As the Prince's counsel declared that my claim could not be heard till the choice of a guardian had been made, and as I now hear that Y. H. has been graciously pleased yourself to assume that office, but decline receiving anyone, I present my humble petition in writing, requesting at the same time your early consideration; for you can easily understand that, relying on a thing as a certainty, it is painful to be so long deprived of it, especially as I am obliged entirely to support an unfortunate sickly brother and his whole family,* which (not computing my own wants) has entirely exhausted my resources, having expected to provide for myself by the payment of my salary. You may perceive the justice of my claims from the fact of my faithfully naming the receipt of the sixty ducats, advanced to me by the late Prince in Prague, the Prince's counsel himself declaring that I might have said nothing about this sum, the late Prince not having mentioned it either to him or to his cashier.

Forgive my being obliged to intrude this affair on you, but necessity compels me to do so. Some days

---

* See a letter to Ries, Nov. 22nd, 1815 :—' He was consumptive for some years, and, in order to make his life easier, I can safely compute what I gave him at 10,000 florins W.W.'

hence I shall take the liberty of making enquiries on the subject from the Prince's counsel, or from anyone Y. H. may appoint.

I remain, most esteemed and illustrious Princess,

Your devoted servant,

LUDWIG VAN BEETHOVEN.

100.

*To Zmeskall.*

Dear Z.,

Forward the accompanying letter to-day without fail to Brunswick, that it may arrive as soon and as safely as possible. Excuse the trouble I give you. I have been again applied to, to send some of my works to Gratz, in Styria, for a concert to be given in aid of the Ursuline convent and its schools : last year they had very large receipts by this means. Including this concert, and one I gave in Carlsbad for the benefit of the sufferers from fire at Baden, three concerts have been given by me, and through me, for benevolent purposes in one year; and yet if I ask a favour, people are as deaf as a post.

Your BEETHOVEN.

I. Letter to Sclowonowitsch (Maître des bureaux des postes) in Cassel. I can no longer do without the books of Tiedge and Frau von der Recke, as I am expected to give some opinion about them.

101.

*To Herr Joseph Varenna,—Gratz.*

My good Sir,

Rode was not quite correct in all that he said of me; my health is not particularly good, and from no fault of my own—my present condition being the most unfortunate of my life. But neither this nor anything in the world shall prevent me from assisting, so far as it lies in my power, the innocent and distressed ladies of your convent by my poor works. I therefore place at your disposal two new Symphonies, a bass Aria with chorus, and several minor Choruses; if you desire again to perform ' Hungaria's Benefactors,' which you gave last year, it is also at your service. Among the Choruses you will find a ' Dervise Chorus,' a capital bait for a mixed public.

In my opinion, your best plan would be to select a day when you could give the ' Mount of Olives,' which has been everywhere performed. This would occupy one half of the concert, and the other half might consist of a new Symphony, the Overtures, and various Choruses, and likewise the above-named bass Aria and Chorus; thus the evening would not be devoid of variety. But you can settle all this more satisfactorily with the aid of your own musical authorities. I think I can guess what you mean about a gratuity for me from a *third person.* Were I in the same position as formerly, I would at once say ' Beethoven never accepts anything

*where the benefit of humanity is concerned;* ' but owing
to my own too great benevolence I am reduced to a
low ebb, the cause of which, however, does not put me
to shame, being combined with other circumstances for
which men devoid of honour and principle are alone to
blame, so I do not hesitate to say that I would not refuse
the contribution of the rich man to whom you allude.*
But there is no question here of any *claim.* If, however, the affair with the *third person* comes to nothing,
pray rest assured that I shall be equally disposed to
confer the same benefit as last year on my friends the
respected Ursuline ladies, and shall at all times be ready
to succour the poor and needy so long as I live. And
now farewell! Write soon, and I will zealously strive to
make all necessary arrangements. My best wishes for
the convent.

I am, with esteem, your friend,

LUDWIG VAN BEETHOVEN.

102.

*To Varenna.*

My excellent V. [Varenna],

I received your letter with much pleasure, but with
much displeasure the 100 florins allotted to me by our

---

* Reichardt, on the 1st March, 1809, writes in his 'Vertraute Briefe :'—
' Beethoven by "a rich third person," as the following letter proves,
meant Louis Buonaparte, who, after abdicating the Dutch throne, lived
in Gratz.'

poor convent ladies; in the meantime I will apply part
of this sum to pay the copyists—the surplus and the
accounts for copying shall be sent to these good ladies.

I never accept anything for such a purpose. I thought
that perhaps the *third person* to whom you alluded
might be the Ex-King of Holland, in which case I
should have had no scruples, under my present circumstances, in accepting a gratuity from him, who has no
doubt taken enough from the Dutch in a less legitimate
way; but as it is, I must decline (though in all friendship) any renewal of this subject.

Let me know whether, were I to come myself to
Gratz, I could give a concert, and what the receipts
would probably be; for Vienna, alas! can no longer
continue my place of abode. Perhaps it is now too late?
but any information from you on the point will be very
welcome.

The works are being copied, and you shall have them
as soon as possible. You may do just what you please
with the Oratorio; where it will be of most use it will
best fulfil my intentions.

I am, with esteem, your obedient

BEETHOVEN.

P. S. Say all that is kind from me to the worthy
Ursuline ladies. I rejoice in being able to serve
them.

## 103.

### *To Zmeskall.*

Confounded, invited guest! *Domanowetz!*—not musical Count, but gobbling Count! dinner Count! supper Count! &c. &c. The Quartett is to be tried over to-day at ten o'clock or half-past, at Lobkowitz's.* His Highness, whose wits are generally astray, is not yet arrived, so pray join us, if you can escape from your Chancery jailer. Herzog is to see you to-day. He intends to take the post of my man-servant; you may agree to give him thirty florins, with his wife *obbligata.* Firing, light, and morning livery found. I must have some one who knows how to cook, for if my food continues as bad as it now is, I shall always be ill. I dine at home to-day, because I get better wine. If you will only order what you like, I very much wish you to come to me. You shall have the wine *gratis,* and of far better quality than what you get at the scoundrelly 'Swan.'

Your very insignificant

BEETHOVEN.

---

* Reichardt, in his 'Vertraute Briefe,' writes:—'The beautiful Quartetts and evening concerts for the Archduke Rudolph still continue at Prince von Lobkowitz's, although the Prince himself is about to join his battalion in Bohemia.' Reichardt, vol. i. p. 182, calls Lobkowitz 'an indefatigable, insatiable, genuine enthusiast for art.'

### 104.

*To Zmeskall.*

I have been constantly indisposed, dear Zmeskall, since I last saw you; in the meantime the servant who lived with you before your present one has applied for my situation. I do not recollect him, but he told me he had been with you, and that you had nothing to say against him, except that he did not dress your hair as you wished. I gave him earnest-money, though only a florin. Supposing you have no other fault to find with the man (and if so I beg you will candidly mention it), I intend to engage him, for you know that it is no object with me to have my hair dressed : it would be more to the purpose if my finances could be dressed, or *re-dressed*. I hope to get an answer from you to-day. If there is no one to open the door to your servant, let him leave the note in the entrance to the left, and should he find no one there either, he must give it to the porter's wife below stairs. May Heaven prosper you in your musical undertakings!

Your BEETHOVEN,
*Miserabilis.*

### 105.

*To Zmeskall.*

Feb. 28, 1813.

Let us leave things as they are for to-day, dear Z., till we meet [and so on about the servant].

Farewell! Carefully guard the fortresses of the realm, which, as you know, are no longer virgins, and have already received many a shot.

Your friend,

BEETHOVEN.

### 106.

#### *To Zmeskall.*

Most worthy Counsellor, Owner of Mines and Lord of Fastnesses in Burgundy and Buda!

Be so good as to let me know how matters stand, as this afternoon at latest I shall take advantage of your reply to my question, by giving my servant warning for this day fortnight. His wages, &c. &c. [The rest relates to his servant.]

### 107.

#### *To Zmeskall.*

April 19, 1813.

My dear Zmeskall,

I have been refused the University Hall. I heard this two days since; but being indisposed yesterday I could not go to see you, nor can I to-day either. We have no resource now but the Kärnthnerthor Theatre, or the one 'an der Wien.' I believe there will only be one concert. If both these fail, we must then have recourse to the Augarten, in which case we ought certainly to give two concerts. Reflect on this, my dear friend, and let me have your opinion. To-morrow the Symphonies may perhaps be tried over at the Archduke's if I am able to go out, of which I will apprise you.

Your friend,<br>
BEETHOVEN.

### 108.

### *To Zmeskall.*

Dear Z.,                                    April 23, 1813.

All will go right, the Archduke being resolved to take this Prince *Fizlypuzly* roundly to task. Let me know if you are to dine at the tavern to-day, or where? Pray tell me if ' Sentivany ' is properly spelt, as I wish to write to him at the same time about the Chorus. We must also consult together what day to choose. By the by, be cautious not to mention the intercession of the Archduke, for Prince *Fizlypuzly* is not to be with him till Sunday, and if that evil-minded creditor had any previous hint of the affair, he would still try to evade us.

Yours ever,<br>
BEETHOVEN.

### 109.

### *To Zmeskall.*

April 26, 1813.

Lobkowitz will give me a day on the 15th of May, or after that period, which seems to me scarcely better than none at all, so I am almost disposed to give up all idea of a concert. But the Almighty will no doubt prevent my being utterly ruined.

Yours,<br>
BEETHOVEN.

## 110.

### *To the Archduke Rudolph.*

Baden, May 27, 1813.

I have the honour to inform you of my arrival in Baden, which is indeed still very empty of human beings, but with all the greater luxuriance and full lustre does Nature shine in her enchanting loveliness. Where I fail, or ever have failed, be graciously indulgent towards me, for so many trying occurrences, succeeding each other so closely, have really almost bewildered me; still I am convinced that the resplendent beauties of Nature here, and the charming environs, will gradually restore my spirits, and a double share of tranquillity be my portion, as by my stay here I likewise fulfil the wishes of Y. R. H. Would that my desire soon to hear that Y. R. H. is fully restored were equally fulfilled! This is indeed my warmest wish, and how much I grieve that I cannot at this moment contribute to your recovery by means of *my* art! This is reserved for the goddess Hygeia alone, and I, alas! am only a poor mortal, who commends himself to Y. R. H., and sincerely hopes soon to be permitted to wait on you.

[K.]

## 111.

### *To the Archduke Rudolph.*

Vienna, July 24, 1813.

From day to day I have been expecting to return to Baden; in the meantime, the discords that detain me here may possibly be resolved by the end of the ensuing week. To me a residence in a town during the summer is misery, and when I also remember that I am thus prevented waiting on Y. R. H., it is still more vexatious and annoying. It is, in fact, the Lobkowitz and Kinsky affairs that keep me here. Instead of pondering over a number of bars, I am obliged constantly to reflect on the number of peregrinations I am forced to make; but for this, I could scarcely endure to the end. Y. R. H. has no doubt heard of Lobkowitz's misfortunes,* which are much to be regretted; but after all, to be rich is no such great happiness! It is said that Count Fries alone paid 1,900 gold ducats to Duport, for which he had the security of the ancient Lobkowitz house. The details are beyond all belief. I hear that Count Rasumowsky † intends to go to Baden, and to take his Quartett with him, which is really very pretty, and I have no doubt that Y. R. H. will be much pleased with it. I know no more charming enjoyment in the country than quartett music. I beg Y. R. H. will accept my

* Prince Lobkowitz's 'misfortunes' probably refer to the great pecuniary difficulties which befell this music and pomp-loving Prince several years before his death. Beethoven seems to have made various attempts to induce the Prince to continue the payment of his share of the salary agreed on, though these efforts were long fruitless. The subject, however, appears to have been again renewed in 1816, for on the 8th of March in this year Beethoven writes to Ries to say that his salary consists of 3,400 florins E. S., and this sum he received till his death.

† Those who played in Count Rasumowsky's Quartetts, to whom Beethoven dedicated various compositions, were the *virtuosi* Schuppanzigh (1st), Sina (2nd violin), Linke (violoncello), Weiss (violin).

heartfelt wishes for your health, and also compassionate
me for being obliged to pass my time here under such
disagreeable circumstances.  But I will strive to compensate twofold in Baden for what you have lost.

[K.]

## 112.

### To the Archduke Rudolph.

1813.*

I beg to enquire whether, being in some degree restored, I am to wait on you this evening?  I at the
same time take the liberty to make a humble request.
I was in hopes that by this time, at all events, my
melancholy circumstances would have brightened, but
all continues in its old state, so I must determine on
giving two concerts.†  I find that I am compelled to
give up my former resolution never to give any except
for benevolent purposes; as self-maintenance demands
that I should do so.  The hall of the University would be
the most advantageous and distinguished for my present
object, and my humble request consists in entreating
Y. R. H. to be so gracious as to send a line to the present *Rector Magnificus* of the University, through Baron
Schweiger, which would certainly ensure my getting the
hall.  In the hope of a favourable answer, I remain, &c. &c.

[K.]

* Late in the autumn of 1813.

† The concerts here referred to were given in the University Hall on
the 8th and 12th December, 1813, when the ' Battle of Vittoria' and the
A major Symphony were performed for the first time.  Beethoven himself conducted.

## 113.

### To Freiherr Josef von Schweiger.

Late in the Autumn of 1813.

My dear Friend,

I have to-day applied (by letter) to my gracious master to interest himself in procuring the University Hall for two concerts which I think of giving, and in fact must give, for all remains as it was; always considering you, both in good and evil fortune, my best friend. I suggested to the Duke that you should apply in his name for this favour to the present Rector of the University. Whatever may be the result, let me know H. R. H.'s decision as soon as possible, that I may make further efforts to extricate myself from a position so detrimental to me and to my art. I am coming this evening to the Archduke.

Your friend,

[K.]                                BEETHOVEN.

## 114.

### To Herr von Baumeister.*

Dear Sir,

I request you will send me the parts of the Symphony in A, and likewise my score. His I. H. can have the MS. again, but I require it at present for the music in the Augarten to-morrow. I have just received

* Private Secretary to the Archduke Rudolph.

two tickets, which I send to you, and beg you will make use of them.

I am, with esteem, yours,

L. v. BEETHOVEN.

### 115.

### *To Zmeskall.*

Oct. 9, 1813.

My dear good Z.,

Don't be indignant with me for asking you to address the enclosed letter properly; the person for whom it is intended is constantly complaining that he gets no letters from me. Yesterday I took one myself to the post-office, when I was asked where the letter was meant to go. I see, therefore, that my writing seems to be as little understood as myself. Thence my request to you.

Your BEETHOVEN.

### 116.

### *Letter of Thanks.*

I esteem it my duty to express my gratitude for the great zeal shown by all those artists who so kindly co-operated on the 8th and 12th December [1813] in the concerts given for the benefit of the Austrian and Bavarian soldiers wounded at the battle of Hanau. It was a rare combination of eminent artists, where all were inspired by the wish to be of use to their father-land, and to contribute by the exercise of their talents to the fulfilment of the undertaking, while, regardless of all precedence, they gladly accepted subordinate places.* While an artist like Herr Schuppanzigh was at the head of the first violins, and by his fiery and expressive mode of conducting kindled the zeal of the whole orchestra, Herr Kapellmeister Salieri did not scruple to give the time to the drums and cannonades; Herr Spohr and Herr Mayseder, each worthy from his talents to fill the highest post, played in the second and third rank. Herr Siboni and Herr Giuliani also filled subordinate places. The conducting of the whole was only assigned to me from the music being my own composition; had it been that of anyone else, I would willingly, like Herr Hummel, have taken my place at the big drum, as the only feeling that pervaded all our hearts was true love for our fatherland, and the wish cheerfully to devote our powers to those who had sacrificed so much for us. Particular thanks are due to Herr Maelzel, inasmuch as he first suggested the idea of this concert, and the most troublesome part of the enterprise, the requisite arrangements, management, and regulations, devolved on him. I more especially thank him for giving me an opportunity by this concert of fulfilling a wish I have long cherished, to compose for such a benevolent object (exclusive of the works already made over to him) a comprehensive work more adapted to the present times, to be laid on the altar of my

* The A major Symphony and 'Wellington's Victory at Vittoria' were performed.

fatherland.*   As a notice is to be published of all those
who assisted on this occasion, the public will be enabled
to judge of the noble self-denial exercised by a mass
of the greatest artists, working together with the same
benevolent object in view.

LUDWIG VAN BEETHOVEN.

117.

*To the Archduke Rudolph.*†

1814.

I beg you will send me the score of the 'Final
Chorus' ‡ for half a day, as the theatrical score is so
badly written.

[K.]

118.

*To the Archduke Rudolph.*

1814.

Having only so recently received the score of the
'Final Chorus,' I must ask you to excuse your getting
it back so late.   The best thing H. R. H. can do is to
have it transcribed, for in its present form the score is
of no use.   I would have brought it myself, but I have

---

* 'Obsolete' is written in pencil by Beethoven.

† The spring of 1814.

‡ The 'Schlusschor,' the score of which Beethoven requests the Archduke to send him, is in all probability the Finale 'Germania! Germania!'
intended for Treitschke's Operetta 'Die gute Nachricht,' which refers to
the taking of Paris by the Allies, and was performed for the first time at
Vienna in the Kärnthnerthor Theatre on the 11th April, 1814.   The same
'Final Chorus' was substituted for another of Beethoven's ('Es ist voll-
bracht') in Treitschke's Operetta 'Die Ehrenpforten,' first given on the
15th July, 1815, in the Kärnthnerthor Theatre. . Both these choruses are
printed in score in Breitkopf & Härtel's edition of Beethoven's works.

been laid up with a cold since last Sunday, which is most severe, and obliges me to be very careful, being so much indisposed. I never feel greater satisfaction than when Y. R. H. derives any pleasure through me. I hope very soon to be able to wait on you myself, and in the meantime I pray that you will keep me in remembrance.

[K.]

### 119.

#### To the Archduke Rudolph.

1814.

The song 'Germania' belongs to the whole world who sympathise with the subject, and to you beyond all others, just as I myself am wholly yours. I wish you a good journey to Palermo.

[K.]

### 120.

#### To Treitschke.

March 1814.

My dear, worthy T.,

I have read with the greatest satisfaction your amendments of the Opera [*Fidelio*, which was about to be again performed]. It has decided me once more to rebuild the desolate ruins of an ancient fortress.

Your friend,

BEETHOVEN.

### 121.

#### To Treitschke.

The affair of the Opera is the most troublesome in the world, and there is scarcely one part of it which quite satisfies me now, and that I have not been obliged to *amend by something more satisfactory.* But what a difference between this, and giving one's self up to freely flowing thought and inspiration!

## 122.

### To Treitschke.

1814.

I request, my dear T., that you will send me the score of the song [in 'Fidelio,' *Geld ist eine schöne Sache*], that the interpolated notes may be transcribed in all the instrumental parts; though I shall not take it at all amiss if you prefer that Girowetz or any other person, perhaps Weinmüller [who sang the part of Rocco], should do so. This I have nothing to say against, but I will not suffer my composition to be altered by any-one whatever, be he who he may.

I am, with high consideration,

Your obedient

BEETHOVEN.

## 123.

### To Count Moritz Lichnowsky.*

My dear Count,

If you wish to attend our council [about the altera-tions in 'Fidelio'], I beg to inform you that it assembles

---

* The mention of Weinmüller decides the date of this note, as it was in the spring of 1814 that he, together with the singers Saal and Vogl, brought about the revival of 'Fidelio.'

this afternoon at half-past three o'clock, in the Spiel-
mann Haus, auf dem Graben, No. 188, 4th Etage, at
Herr Weinmüller's. I shall be very glad if you have
leisure to be present.

### 124.

### *To Count Moritz Lichnowsky.**

My dear, victorious, and yet sometimes nonplussed (?)
Count! I hope that you rested well, most precious
and charming of all Counts! Oh! most beloved and
unparalleled Count! most fascinating and prodigious
Count!

* In Schindler's 'Beethoven's Nachlass' there is also an autograph
Canon of Beethoven's in F major, $\frac{6}{8}$, on Count Lichnowsky, on the words,
*Bester Herr Graf, Sie sind ein Schaf,* written (according to Schindler) Feb.

(*To be repeated at pleasure.*)

At what hour shall we call on Walter to-day? My going or not depends entirely on you.

Your BEETHOVEN.


### 125.

#### *To the Archduke Rudolph.*

1814.

I hope you forgive me for not having come to you. Your displeasure would be totally undeserved, and I will amply compensate for lost time in a few days. My Opera

20th, 1823, in the coffee-house, 'Die Goldne Birne,' in the Landstrasse, where Beethoven usually went every evening, though he generally slipped in by the back door.

of 'Fidelio'* is again to be performed, which gives me
a great deal to do ; moreover, though I look well, I am
not so in reality.   The arrangements for my second concert † are partly completed.   I must write something new
for Mdlle. Milder.‡   Meanwhile it is a consolation to
me to hear that Y. R. H. is so much better.   I hope
I am not too sanguine in thinking that I shall soon
be able to contribute towards this.   I have taken the
liberty to apprise my Lord Falstaff § that he is ere
long to have the honour of appearing before Y. R. H.
[K.]

### 126.
### *To the Archduke Rudolph.*

Vienna, July 14, 1814.

Whenever I enquire about you I hear nothing but
good news.   As for my own insignificant self, I have
been hitherto hopelessly detained in Vienna, and unable to approach Y. R. H. ; I am also thus deprived

---

* Letters 125 and 126 refer to the revival of the Opera of 'Fidelio,'
which had not been given since 1806, and was not again produced on
the stage till the 23rd May, 1814, in the Kärnthnerthor Theatre. Beethoven's benefit took place on the 8th July, two newly composed pieces
being inserted.

† Beethoven gave a concert on the 2nd January, 1814, when 'Wellington's Victory' was performed, and on the 26th March another for
the benefit of the Theatrical Fund, at which the 'Overture to Egmont'
and 'Wellington's Victory' were given, directed by Beethoven himself.

‡ Anna Milder, Royal Court opera singer, a pupil of Vogl's, who first
sang the part of Leonore in 'Fidelio.'

§ By 'my Lord Falstaff' he means the corpulent violinist Schuppanzigh.

of the enjoyment of beautiful Nature, so dear to me. The directors of the theatre are so *conscientious,* that, contrary to their faithful promise, they have again given my Opera of ' Fidelio,' without thinking of giving me any share in the receipts. They would have exhibited the same commendable good faith a second time, had I not been on the watch like a French customhouse officer of other days. At last, after a great many troublesome discussions, it was settled that the Opera of ' Fidelio' should be given on Monday the 18th of July, for my benefit. These *receipts* at this season of the year may more properly be called *deceits* ; but if a work is in any degree successful it often becomes a little feast for the author. To this feast the master invites his illustrious pupil, and hopes—yes! I hope that Y. R. H. will graciously consent to come, and thus add lustre to everything by your presence. It would be a great boon if Y. R. H. would endeavour to persuade the other members of the Imperial family to be present at the representation of my Opera, and I on my part will not fail to take the proper steps on the subject which duty commands. Vogl's illness * enabled me to satisfy my desire to give the part of Pizarro to Forti,† his voice being better suited to it; but owing to this

---

* Joh. Mich. Vogl, born August 10th, 1768, was Court opera singer (tenor) in Vienna from 1794 to 1822; he died November 19th, 1840.

† Forti, born June 8th, 1790, a member of the Royal Court Theatre (a barytone), pensioned off in 1834.

there are daily rehearsals, which cannot fail to have a favourable effect on the performance, but which render it impossible for me to wait upon Y. R. H. before my benefit. Pray give this letter your favourable consideration, and think graciously of me.

[K.]

## 127.

### *Deposition.*

1814.

I voluntarily presented Maelzel *gratis* with a 'Battle Symphony' for his panharmonica. After having kept it for some time, he brought me back the score, which he had already begun to engrave, saying that he wished it to be harmonised for a full orchestra. The idea of a battle had already occurred to me, which, however, could not be performed on his panharmonica. We agreed to select this and some more of my works [see No. 116] to be given at the concert for the benefit of disabled soldiers. At that very time I became involved in the most frightful pecuniary difficulties. Forsaken by everyone in Vienna, and in daily expectation of remittances, &c., Maelzel offered me fifty gold ducats, which I accepted, saying that I would either repay them, or allow him to take the work to London (provided I did not go there myself with him), referring him to an English publisher for payment.

I got back from him the score written for the panharmonica. The concerts then took place, and during

that time Herr Maelzel's designs and character were first fully revealed. Without my consent, he stated on the bills of the concert that the work was *his property*. Indignant at this, I insisted on his destroying these bills. He then stated that I had given it to him as a friendly act, because he was going to London. To this I did not object, believing that I had reserved the right to state the conditions on which the work should be his own. I remember that when the bills were being printed, I violently opposed them, but the time was too short, as I was still writing the work. In all the fire of inspiration, and absorbed in my composition, I scarcely thought at all on the subject. Immediately after the first concert in the University Hall, I was told on all sides, and by people on whom I could rely, that Maelzel had everywhere given out he had paid me 400 gold ducats for the Symphony. I sent what follows to a newspaper, but the editor would not insert it, as Maelzel stands well with them all. As soon as the first concert was over, I repaid Maelzel his fifty ducats, declaring that having discovered his real character, nothing should ever induce me to travel with him ; justly indignant that, without consulting me, he had stated in the bills that all the arrangements for the concert were most defective. His own despicable want of patriotism too is proved by the following expressions :—
' I care nothing at all about L. ; if it is only said in London that people have paid ten gulden for admission

here, that is all I care about;—the wounded are nothing
to me.'   Moreover, I told him that he might take the
work to London on certain conditions, which I would
inform him of.  He then asserted that it was a *friendly
gift*, and made use of this phrase in the newspapers
after the second concert, without giving me the most
remote hint on the subject.   As Maelzel is a rude,
churlish man, entirely devoid of education or cultivation, it is easy to conceive the tenour of his conduct to
me during this time, which still further irritated me.
Who could bear to be forced to bestow a *friendly gift* on
such a man ?   I was offered an opportunity to send the
work to the Prince Regent [afterwards George IV.].  It
was therefore quite impossible for me to *give away the
work unconditionally.*

He then called on a mutual friend to make proposals.
He was told on what day to return for an answer, but
he never appeared, set off on his travels, and performed
the work in Munich.   How did he obtain it ?   He
could not possibly *steal* it ; but Herr Maelzel had
several of the parts for some days in his house, and he
caused the entire work to be harmonised by some obscure musical journeyman, and is now hawking it about
the world.  Herr Maelzel promised me ear-trumpets.  I
harmonised the ' Battle Symphony' for his panharmonica
from a wish to keep him to his word.  The ear-trumpets
came at last, but were not of the service to me that I
expected.   For this slight trouble Herr Maelzel, after

my having arranged the 'Battle Symphony' for a full orchestra, and composed a battle piece in addition, declared that I ought to have made over these works to him as *his own exclusive property.* Even allowing that I am in some degree obliged to him for the ear-trumpets, this is entirely balanced by his having made at least 500 gulden in Munich by my mutilated or stolen battle piece. He has therefore paid himself in full. He had actually the audacity to say here that he was in possession of the battle piece; in fact he showed it, written out, to various persons. I did not believe this; and, in fact, with good reason, as the whole is not by me, but compiled by some one else. Indeed the credit he assumes for the work should alone be sufficient compensation.

The secretary at the War Office made no allusion whatever to me, and yet every work performed at both concerts was of my composition.

Herr Maelzel thinks fit to say that he has delayed his visit to London on account of the battle piece, which is a mere subterfuge. He stayed to finish his patch-work, as the first attempt did not succeed.

BEETHOVEN.

## 128.

*To Herr J. Kauka, Doctor of Laws in Prague, in the Kingdom of Bohemia.*

The Summer of 1814.

A thousand thanks, my esteemed Kauka. At last I meet with a *legal representative* and a *man,* who can both write and think without using unmeaning formulas. You can scarcely imagine how I long for the end of this affair, as it not only interferes with my domestic expenditure, but is injurious to me in various ways. You know yourself that a sensitive spirit ought not to be fettered by miserable anxieties, and much that might render my life happy is thus abstracted from it. Even my inclination and the duty I assigned myself, to serve suffering humanity by means of my art, I have been obliged to limit, and must continue to do so.\*

I write nothing about our monarchs and monarchies, for the newspapers give you every information on these subjects.† The intellectual realm is the most precious in my eyes, and far above all temporal and spiritual monarchies. Write to me, however, what you wish *for yourself* from my poor musical capabilities, that I may, in so far as it lies in my power, supply something for your

---

\* He supported a consumptive brother and his wife and child.

† At the Vienna Congress Beethoven was received with much distinction by the potentates present.

own musical sense and feeling. Do you not require all the papers connected with the Kinsky case? If so I will send them to you, as they contain most important testimony, which, indeed, I believe you read when with me. Think of me, and do not forget that you represent a disinterested artist in opposition to a niggardly family. How gladly do men withhold from the poor artist in one respect *what they pay him in another*, and there is no longer a Zeus with whom an artist can invite himself to feast on ambrosia. Strive, my dear friend, to accelerate the tardy steps of justice. Whenever I feel myself elevated high, and in happy moments revel in my artistic sphere, circumstances drag me down again, and none more than these two lawsuits. You too have your disagreeable moments, though with the views and capabilities I know you to possess, especially in your profession, I could scarcely have believed this; still I must recall your attention to myself. I have drunk to the dregs a cup of bitter sorrow, and already earned martyrdom in art through my beloved artistic disciples and colleagues. I beg you will think of me every day, and imagine it to be an *entire world*, for it is really asking rather too much of you to think of so humble an *individual* as myself.

I am, with the highest esteem and friendship,

Your obedient

Ludwig van Beethoven.

### 129.

*Address and Appeal to London Artists by L. van Beethoven.*

Vienna, July 25, 1814.

Herr Maelzel, now in London, on his way thither performed my 'Battle Symphony' and 'Wellington's Battle of Vittoria' in Munich, and no doubt he intends to produce them at London concerts, as he wished to do in Frankfort. This induces me to declare that I never in any way made over or transferred the said works to Herr Maelzel; that no one possesses a copy of them, and that the only one verified by me I sent to His Royal Highness the Prince Regent of England. The performance of these works, therefore, by Herr Maelzel is either an imposition on the public, as the above declaration proves that he does not possess them, or if he does, he has been guilty of a breach of faith towards me, inasmuch as he must have got them in a surreptitious manner.

But even in the latter case the public will still be deluded, for the works that Herr Maelzel performs under the titles of 'Wellington's Battle of Vittoria' and 'Battle Symphony' are beyond all doubt spurious and mutilated, as he never had any portion of either of these works of mine, except some of the parts for a few days.

This suspicion becomes a certainty from the testimony of various artists here, whose names I am authorised to give if necessary. These gentlemen state that Herr Maelzel, before he left Vienna, declared that he was in possession of these works, and showed various portions, which, however, as I have already proved, must be counterfeit. The question whether Herr Maelzel be capable of doing me such an injury, is best solved by the following fact. In the public papers he named himself as sole giver of the concert on behalf of our wounded soldiers, whereas my works alone were performed there, and yet he made no allusion whatsoever to me.

I therefore appeal to the London musicians not to permit such a grievous wrong to be done to their fellow-artist by Herr Maelzel's performance of the ' Battle of Vittoria ' and the ' Battle Symphony,' and also to prevent the London public being so shamefully imposed upon.

### 130.

### *To Dr. Kauka.*

Vienna, August 22, 1814.

You have shown a feeling for harmony, and you can resolve a great discord in my life, which causes me much discomfort, into more pleasing melody, if you will. I shortly expect to hear something of what you understand is likely to happen, as I eagerly anticipate the result of this most *unjust* affair with the Kinskys. When the Princess was here, she seemed to be well disposed towards me; still I do not know how it will

end. In the meantime I must restrict myself in everything, and await with entire confidence what is *right-
fully my own* and *legally devolves on me*, and though
unforeseen occurrences caused changes in this matter,
still two witnesses recently bore testimony to the wish
of the deceased Prince that my appointed salary in
*Banco Zettel* should be paid in *Einlösung Schein*
making up the original sum, and the Prince himself
gave me sixty gold ducats *on account* of my claim.

Should the affair turn out badly for me by the conduct of the Kinsky family, I will publish it in every
newspaper, to their disgrace. If there had been an heir,
and the facts had been told to him *in all their truth*
just as I narrated them, I am convinced that he would
at once have adopted the words and deeds of his pre-
decessor. Has Dr. Wolf [the previous advocate] shown
you the papers, or shall I make you acquainted with
them? As I am by no means sure that this letter will
reach you safely, I defer sending you the pianoforte
arrangement of my Opera 'Fidelio,' which is ready to
be despatched.

I hope, in accordance with your usual friendliness,
soon to hear from you. I am also writing to Dr. Wolf
(who certainly does not treat anyone *wolfishly*), in order
not to arouse his *passion*, so that he may have *compassion* on me, and neither take my purse nor my life.

I am, with esteem, your true friend,

LUDWIG VAN BEETHOVEN.

131.

*To Count Moritz Lichnowsky.*

Baden, Sept. 21, 1841*.

Most esteemed Count and Friend,

I unluckily only got your letter yesterday.   A thousand thanks for ·your remembrance of me. Pray express my gratitude also to your charming Princess Christiane [wife of Prince Carl Lichnowsky].   I had a delightful walk yesterday with a friend in the Brühl, and in the course of our friendly chat you were particularly mentioned, and lo! and behold! on my return I found your kind letter.   I see you are resolved to continue to load me with benefits.

As I am unwilling you should suppose that a step I have already taken is prompted by your recent favours, or by any motive of the sort, I must tell you that a Sonata of mine [Op. 90] is about to appear, *dedicated to you.*   I wished to give you a surprise, as this dedication has been long designed for you, but your letter of yesterday induces me to name the fact.   I required no new motive thus publicly to testify my sense of your friendship and kindness.   But as for anything approaching to a gift in return, you would only distress me, by thus totally misinterpreting my intentions, and I should at once decidedly refuse such a thing.

I beg to kiss the hand of the Princess for her kind message and all her goodness to me.   *Never have I*

* The date reversed, as written by Beethoven, is here given.

*forgotten what I owe to you all,* though an unfortunate combination of circumstances prevented my testifying this as I could have wished.

From what you tell me about Lord Castlereagh, I think the matter in the best possible train. If I were to give an opinion on the subject, I should say that Lord Castlereagh ought to hear the work given here before writing to Wellington. I shall soon be in Vienna, when we can consult together about a grand concert. Nothing is to be effected at Court; I made the application, but —but—

al = lein    al = lein    al = lein

*Silentium ! ! !*

Farewell, my esteemed friend; pray continue to esteem me worthy of your friendship.

Yours,

BEETHOVEN.

A thousand compliments to the illustrious Princess.


132.

*To the Archduke Rudolph.*

1814.

I perceive that Y. R. H. wishes to try the effect of my music even upon horses.* We shall see whether its

---

* A tournament was held on the 23rd November, 1814, in the Royal Riding School. Beethoven was probably requested by the Archduke to compose some music for it, which, however, has not been traced.

influence will cause the riders to throw some clever sum-
mersets. Ha! ha! I can't help laughing at Y. R. H.
thinking of me on such an occasion ; for which I shall
remain so long as I live, &c. &c. &c. The horse music
that Y. R. H. desires shall set off to you full gallop.

[K.]

### 133.

### *To the Archduke Rudolph.*

1814,

It is impossible for me to-day to wait on you, much as
I wish it. I am despatching the work on Wellington's
victory * to London. Such matters have their appointed
and fixed time, which cannot be delayed without final
loss. To-morrow I hope to be able to call on Y. R. H.

[K.]

### 134.

### *To the Archduke Rudolph.*

(In a different hand) Dec. 1814.

I really feel that I can never deserve your goodness
towards me. I beg to offer my most respectful thanks
for Y. R. H.'s gracious intervention in my affairs at
Prague. I will punctually attend to the score of the
Cantata.† I trust Y. R. H. will forgive my not having

---

* The Cantata 'Der glorreiche Augenblick,' the poetry by Dr. Alois
Weissenbach, set to music by Beethoven for chorus and orchestra (Op.
136), was first given in Vienna on the 29th November, 1814, and repeated
on the 2nd December.

† What concert Beethoven alludes to I cannot discover, but no mention of it being made in the very exact 'Allgemeine Leipziger Musikalische Zeitung,' it appears not to have taken place.

yet been to see you. After the concert for the poor, comes one in the theatre, equally for the benefit of the *impresario in angustia,* for they have felt some just shame, and have let me off with one-third and one-half of the usual charges. I have now some fresh work on hand, and then there is a new Opera to be begun,* the subject of which I am about to decide on. Moreover, I am again far from well, but a few days hence I will wait on Y. R. H. If I could be of any service to Y. R. H., the most eager and anxious wish of my life would be fulfilled.

[K.]

### 135.

#### To the Archduke Rudolph.

1814.

My warmest thanks for your present.† I only regret that you could not participate in the music. I have now the honour to send you the score of the Cantata [see No. 134]. Y. R. H. can keep it for some days, and afterwards I shall take care that it is copied for you as soon as possible.

I feel still quite exhausted from fatigue and worry, pleasure and delight !—all combined ! I shall have the honour of waiting on you in the course of a few days.

* The new Opera with the subject of which Beethoven was occupied was no doubt Treitschke's 'Romulus.'

† The present he refers to was probably for the concert of November 29th or December 2nd, 1814.

I hope to hear favourable accounts of Y. R. H.'s health. How gladly would I sacrifice many nights, were it in my power to restore you entirely!

[K.]

## 136.

### To the Archduke Rudolph.

1814.*

I see with real pleasure that I may dismiss all fears for your wellbeing. As for myself, I hope (always feeling happy when able to give you any pleasure) that my health is also rapidly recruiting, when I intend forthwith to compensate both you and myself for the *pauses* that have occurred. As for Prince Lobkowitz, his *pauses* with me still continue, and I fear he will never again come in at the right place; and in Prague (good heavens! with regard to Prince Kinsky's affair) they scarcely as yet know what a figured bass is, for they sing in slow, long-drawn choral notes; some of these sustained through sixteen bars ⊨══╡. As all these discords seem likely to be very slowly resolved, it is best to bring forward only those which we can ourselves resolve, and to give up the rest to inevitable fate. Allow me once more to express my delight at the recovery of Y. R. H.

[K.]

* 1814 or 1815. Prince Lobkowitz was still alive at that time (died December 21st, 1816).

## 137.

### *To the Archduke Rudolph.*

1814.

As you were so kind as to let me know through Count Troyer * that you would write a few lines on my affairs in Prague to the *Oberstburggraf* Count Kolowrat, I take the liberty to enclose my letter to Count K.; I do not believe that it contains anything to which Y. R. H. will take exception. There is no chance of my being allowed payment in *Einlösung Schein,* for, in spite of all the proofs, the guardians cannot be persuaded to consent to this; still it is to be hoped that by the friendly steps we have meanwhile had recourse to, *extrajudicially,* a more favourable result may be obtained—as, for instance, the rate of the scale to be higher. If, however, Y. R. H. will either write a few words yourself, or cause it to be done in your name, the affair will certainly be *much accelerated,* which induces me earnestly to entreat Y. R. H. to perform your gracious promise to me. This affair has now gone on for three years, and is still—undecided.

[K.]

## 138.

### *To the Archduke Rudolph.*

1814.

I have again for a fortnight past been afflicted with severe headaches, though constantly hoping to get better, but in vain. Now, however, that the weather

* Count Ferdinand Troyer was one of the Archduke's chamberlains.

is improved, my physician promises me a speedy cure.
Though as each day I expected to be the last of my
suffering, I did not write to you on the subject; besides,
I thought that Y. R. H. probably did not require me,
as it is so long since Y. R. H. sent for me. During the
festivities in honour of the Princess of Baden,* and
the injury to Y. R. H.'s finger, I began to work very
assiduously, and as the fruit of this, among others, is
a new pianoforte Trio.† Myself very much occupied,
I had no idea that I had incurred the displeasure of
Y. R. H., though I now begin almost to think this to
be the case. In the meantime I hope soon to be able
to present myself before your tribunal.

[K.]

### 139.

#### To the Archduke Rudolph.

1814.

I beg you will be so good as to let me have the Trio
in B flat with all the parts, and also both parts of
the violin Sonata in G,‡ as I must have them written

* The festivities in honour of the Princess of Baden were probably
during the Congress, 1814.

† The new Trio, if the one in B flat for the pianoforte, violin, and
violoncello, Op. 97, was first performed on the 11th April, 1814, in
the hall of the 'Komischer Kaiser.' Letter 139 also mentions this Trio,
composed in 1811 and published in July 1816.

‡ The Sonata for pianoforte and violin in G major, Op. 96, was purchased by Haslinger, April 1st, 1815, and published the end of July
1816. It was composed in 1814—perhaps in 1813. Thayer thinks in
1810.

out for myself with all speed, not being able to hunt out my own scores among so many others. I hope that this detestable weather has had no bad effect on Y. R. H.'s health; I must own that it rather deranges me. In three or four days at least I shall have the honour to restore both works to their proper place.

Do the musical pauses still continue?

[K.]

### 140.

### *To Herr Kauka.*

Vienna, Jan. 11, 1815.

My good, worthy K.,

I received Baron Pasqualati's letter to-day, by which I perceive that you wish me to defer any fresh measures. In the meantime all the necessary papers are lodged with Pasqualati, so be so good as to inform him that he must delay taking any further steps. To-morrow a council is to be held here, and you and P. shall learn the result probably to-morrow evening. Meanwhile I wish you to look through the paper I sent to the Court through Pasqualati, and read the appendix carefully. You will then see that Wolf and others have not given you correct information.

One thing is certain, that there are sufficient proofs *for anyone who wishes to be convinced.* How could it ever occur to me *to think of written legal testimony* with such a man as Kinsky, whose integrity and generosity were everywhere acknowledged? I remain, with the warmest affection and esteem,

In haste,

Your friend,

B.

141.

*To Herr Kauka.*

1815.

My dear and esteemed K.,

What can I think, or say, or feel? As for W. [Wolf], it seems to me that he not only showed *his weak points*, but gave himself no trouble to conceal them. It is impossible that he can have drawn up his statement in accordance with all the actual evidence he had. The order on the Treasury about the rate of exchange was given by Kinsky previous to his consent to pay me my salary in *Einlösung Schein*, as the documents prove; indeed it is only necessary to examine the date to show this, so the first instruction is of importance. The *species facti* prove that I was more than six months absent from Vienna. As I was not anxious to get the money, I allowed the affair to stand over, so the Prince thus forgot to recall his former order to the Treasury, but that he neither forgot his promise to me, nor to Varnhagen [an officer] in my behalf, is evident by the testimony of Herr von Oliva, to whom shortly before his departure from hence—and indeed into another world—he repeated his promise, making an appointment to see him when he should return to Vienna, in order to arrange the matter with the Treasury, which of course was prevented by his untimely death.

The testimony of the officer Varnhagen is accompanied by a document (he being at present with the Russian army), in which he states that he is prepared to *take his oath* on the affair. The evidence of Herr Oliva is also to the effect that he is willing to confirm his evidence by oath before the Court. As I have sent away the testimony of Col. Count Bentheim, I am not sure of its tenour, but I believe the Count also says that he is prepared at any time to make an affidavit on the matter in Court, and I am myself *ready to swear before the Court* that Prince Kinsky said to me in Prague, 'he thought it only fair to me that my salary should be paid in *Einlösung Schein*.' These were his own words.

He gave me himself sixty gold ducats in Prague, on account (good for about 600 florins), as, owing to my state of health, I could remain no longer, and set off for Töplitz. The Prince's word was *sacred* in my eyes, never having heard anything of him to induce me either to bring two witnesses with me, or to ask him for any written pledge. I see from all this that Dr. Wolf has miserably mismanaged the business, and has not made you sufficiently acquainted with the papers.

Now as to the step I have just taken. The Archduke Rudolph asked me some time since whether the Kinsky affair was yet terminated, having probably heard something of it. I told him that it looked very bad, as I knew nothing, absolutely nothing, of the matter. He offered to write himself, but desired me to add a memorandum, and also to make him acquainted with all the papers connected with the Kinsky case. After having informed himself on the affair, he wrote to the *Oberstburggraf*, and enclosed my letter to him.

The *Oberstburggraf* answered both the Duke and myself immediately. In the letter to me he said ' that I was to present a petition to the Provincial Court of Justice in Prague along with all the proofs, whence it would be forwarded to him, and that he would do his utmost to further my cause.' He also wrote in the most polite terms to the Archduke ; indeed, he expressly said ' that he was thoroughly cognizant of the late Prince Kinsky's intentions with regard to me and this affair, and that I might present a petition,' &c. The Archduke instantly sent for me, and desired me to prepare the document and to show it to him ; he also thought that I ought to solicit payment in *Einlösung Schein*, as there was ample proof, if not in strictly legal form, of the intentions of the Prince, and no one could doubt that if he had survived he would have adhered to his promise. If he [the Archduke] were this day the heir, *he would demand no other proofs than those already furnished.* I sent this paper to Baron Pasqualati, who is kindly to present it himself to the Court. Not till after the affair

had gone so far did Dr. Adlersburg receive a letter from
Dr. Wolf, in which he mentioned that he had made a
claim for 1,500 florins. As we have come so far as 1,500
florins with the *Oberstburggraf*, we may possibly get
on to 1,800 florins. I do not esteem this any *favour*,
for the late Prince was one of those who urged me most
to refuse a salary of 600 gold ducats per annum, offered
to me from Westphalia; and he said at the time ' that
he was resolved I should have no chance of eating hams
in Westphalia.' Another summons to Naples somewhat
later I equally declined, and I am entitled to demand a
fair compensation for the loss I incurred. If the salary
were to be paid in bank-notes, what should I get? Not
400 florins in *Conventionsgeld!!!* in lieu of such a
salary as 600 ducats! There are ample proofs for those
who wish to act justly; and what does the *Einlösung
Schein* now amount to??!!! It is even at this moment no equivalent for what I refused. This affair was
pompously announced in all the newspapers while I
was nearly reduced to beggary. The intentions of the
Prince are evident, and in my opinion the family are
bound to act in accordance with them unless they wish
to be disgraced. Besides, the revenues have rather increased than diminished by the death of the Prince, so
there is no sufficient ground for curtailing my salary.

I received your friendly letter yesterday, but am too
weary at this moment to write all that I feel towards
you. I can only commend my case to your sagacity. It

appears that the *Oberstburggraf* is the chief person, so what he wrote to the Archduke must be kept a profound secret, for it might not be advisable that anyone should know of it but you and Pasqualati. You have sufficient cause on looking through the papers to show how improperly Dr. Wolf has conducted the affair, and that another course of action is necessary. I rely on your friendship to act as you think best for my interests.

Rest assured of my warmest thanks, and pray excuse my writing more to-day, for a thing of this kind is very fatiguing—more so than the greatest musical undertaking. My heart has found something for you to which yours will respond, and this you shall soon receive.

Do not forget me, poor tormented creature that I am! and *act for me* and *effect for me* all that is possible.

With high esteem, your true friend,

BEETHOVEN.

142.

*To Herr Kauka.*

Vienna, Jan. 14, 1815.

My good and worthy K.,

The long letter I enclose was written when we were disposed to claim the 1,800 florins. Baron Pasqualati's last letter, however, again made me waver, and Dr. Adlersburg advised me to adhere to the steps already taken; but as Dr. Wolf writes that he has offered in your name to accept 1,500 florins a year, I beg you will at least make every effort to get that sum. For this purpose I send you the long letter written before we received Baron P.'s dissuasive one, as you may discover in it many reasons for demanding *at least* the 1,500 florins.  The Archduke, too, has written a second time to the *Oberstburggraf*, and we may conclude from his previous reply that he will certainly exert himself, and that we shall at all events succeed in getting the 1,500 florins.

Farewell! I cannot write another syllable; such things exhaust me.  May your friendship accelerate this affair!—if it ends badly, then I must leave Vienna, because I could not possibly live on my income, for here things have come to such a pass that everything has risen to the highest price, and that price must be paid. The two last concerts I gave cost me 1,508 florins, and had it not been for the Empress's munificent present I should scarcely have derived any profit whatever.

Your faithful friend,

BEETHOVEN.

143.*

*To the Honourable Members of the Landrecht.*

Vienna, 1815.

Gentlemen,

Quite ignorant of law proceedings, and believing that all claims on an inheritance could not fail to be

* See No. 94.  On the 18th January, 1815, the Court of Justice at Prague decreed that the trustees of Prince Kinsky's estate should pay

liquidated, I sent to my lawyer in Prague [Dr. Kauka] the contract signed by the Archduke Rudolph, Prince Lobkowitz, and Prince von Kinsky, in which these illus· trious personages agreed to settle on me an annual allowance of 4,000 florins. My constant efforts to obtain a settlement of my claim, and also, as I am bound to admit, my reproaches to Dr. Kauka for not conducting the affair properly (his application to the guardians having proved fruitless) no doubt prompted him to have recourse to law.

None but those who are fully aware of my esteem for the deceased Prince, can tell how repugnant it is to my feelings to appear as a complainant against my benefactor.

Under these circumstances, I have recourse to a shorter path, in the conviction that the guardians of the Prince's estate will be disposed to mark their appreciation of art, and also their desire to fulfil the engagements of the late Prince. According to the terms of the contract in question, the Archduke Rudolph, Prince Lobkowitz, and Prince v. Kinsky granted me these 4,000 florins until I should obtain a situation of equal value; and further, if by misfortune or old age I was prevented exercising my art, these distinguished contracting parties

to L. v. Beethoven the sum of 1,200 florins W.W. from November 3rd, 1812, instead of the original written agreement of 1,800 florins. Dr. Constant, of Wurzbach, in his 'Biographical Austrian Lexicon,' states that Beethoven dedicated his splendid song 'An die Hoffnung,' Op. 94, to Princess Kinsky, wife of Prince Ferdinand Kinsky, who died in 1812.

secured this pension to me for life, while I, in return, pledged myself not to leave Vienna.

This promise was generous, and equally generous was its fulfilment, for no difficulty ever occurred, and I was in the peaceful enjoyment of my pension till the Imperial Finance Patent appeared. The consequent alteration in the currency made no difference in the payments of the Archduke Rudolph, for I received his share in *Einlösung Schein*, as I had previously done in bank-notes, without any reference to the new scale. The late illustrious Prince v. Kinsky also at once assured me that his share (1,800 florins) should also be paid in *Einlösung Schein*. As, however, he omitted giving the order to his cashier, difficulties arose on the subject. Although my circumstances are not brilliant, I would not have ventured to bring this claim before the notice of the guardians of the estate, if respectable, upright men had not received the same pledge from the late Prince's own lips, viz., that he would pay my past as well as my future claims in Vienna currency, which is proved by the papers B, C, D, appended to the pleas. Under these circumstances I leave the guardians to judge whether, after so implicitly relying on the promise of the deceased Prince, I have not cause to complain of my delicacy being wounded by the objection advanced by the curators to the witnesses, from their not having been present together at the time the promise was made, which is most distressing to my feelings.

In order to extricate myself from this most disagreeable lawsuit, I take the liberty to give an assurance to the guardians that I am prepared, both as to the past and the future, to be satisfied with the 1,800 florins, Vienna currency ; and I flatter myself that these gentlemen will admit that I on my part make thus no small sacrifice, as it was solely from my esteem for those illustrious Princes that I selected Vienna for my settled abode, at a time when the most advantageous offers were made to me elsewhere.

I therefore request the Court to submit this proposal to the guardians of the Kinsky estates for their opinion, and to be so good as to inform me of the result.

L. V. BEETHOVEN.

144.

*To Baron von Pasqualati.*

January 1815.

My esteemed Friend,

I beg you will kindly send me by the bearer the proper form for the Kinsky receipt (*but sealed*) for 600 florins half-yearly from the month of April. I intend to send the receipt forthwith to Dr. Kauka in Prague,* who on a former occasion procured the money for me so quickly. I will deduct your debt from this, but if it be possible to get the money here before the

---

* This man, now ninety-four years of age and quite blind, was at that time Beethoven's counsel in Prague. Pasqualati was that benefactor of Beethoven's who always kept rooms for him in his house on the Mölker Bastei, and whose kind aid never deserted him to the close of his life.

remittance arrives from Prague, I will bring it at once to you myself.

I remain, with the most profound esteem,

Your sincere friend,

BEETHOVEN.

### 145.

#### To Herr Kauka.

Vienna, Feb. 24, 1815.

My much esteemed K.,

I have repeatedly thanked you through Baron Pasqualati for your friendly exertions on my behalf, and I now beg to express one thousand thanks myself. The intervention of the Archduke could not be very palatable to you, and perhaps has prejudiced you against me. You had already done all that was possible when the Archduke interfered. If this had been the case sooner, and we had not employed that one-sided, or many-sided, or weak-sided Dr. Wolf, then, according to the assurances of the *Oberstburggraf* himself, the affair might have had a still more favourable result. I shall therefore ever and always be grateful to you for your services. The Court now deduct the sixty ducats I mentioned of my own accord, and to which the late Prince never alluded either to his treasurer or anyone else. Where truth could injure me it has been accepted, so why reject it when it could have benefited me? How unfair! Baron Pasqualati requires information from you on various points.

I am again very tired to-day, having been obliged
to discuss many things with poor P. : such matters exhaust me more than the greatest efforts in composition.
It is a new field, the soil of which I ought not to be required to till. This painful business has cost me many
tears and much sorrow. The time draws near when
Princess Kinsky must be written to. Now I must
conclude. How rejoiced shall I be when I can write
you the pure effusions of my heart once more ; and this
I mean to do as soon as I am extricated from all these
troubles. Pray accept again my heartfelt thanks for all
that you have done for me, and continue your regard
for

Your attached friend,

BEETHOVEN.

146.

*To the Archduke Rudolph.*

1815.

I heard yesterday, and it was indeed confirmed by
meeting Count Troyer, that Y. R. H. is now here. I
therefore send the dedication of the Trio [in B flat]
to Y. R. H., whose name is inscribed on it; but all my
works on which I place any value, though the name
does not appear, are equally designed for Y. R. H. I
trust, however, that you will not think I have a motive in saying this; men of high rank being apt to
suspect self-interest in such expressions, and I mean

on this occasion to risk the imputation so far as *appearances* go, by at once asking a favour of Y. R. H. My well-grounded reasons for so doing you will no doubt at once perceive, and graciously vouchsafe to grant my request.   I have been very much indisposed in Baden since the beginning of last October; indeed, from the 5th of October I have been entirely confined to my bed, or to my room, till about a week ago.   I had a very serious inflammatory cold, and am still able to go out very little, which has also been the cause of my not writing to Y. R. H. in Kremsir.   May all the blessings that Heaven can shower upon earth attend you

[K.]

# SECOND PART.

---◆◇◆---

## LIFE'S MISSION.

### 1815 to 1822.

# PART II.

## 147.

*Written in Spohr's Album.* *

Vienna, March 3, 1815.

Kurz,     kurz,     kurz, kurz   ift der Schmerz,   der

Schmerz, e = wig  e  =  =  wig ift die Freu = be,  ift die

Freu = be,  ja die  Freu = be,   e  =  =  =  =  =  =

=  = wig ift die  Freu  =  =  =  =  =  =  =

=  =  =  =  =  =  be.   Kurz,   kurz,

kurz, kurz  ift der Schmerz,  der  Schmerz, der Schmerz, e = wig,

* From the facsimile in Spohr's ' Autobiography,' vol. i.

Whenever, dear Spohr, you chance to find true art and true artists, may you kindly remember

Your friend,

LUDWIG VAN BEETHOVEN.

148.

*To Herr Kauka.*

Vienna, April 8, 1815.

It seems scarcely admissible to be on the friendly terms on which I consider myself with you, and yet to be on such unfriendly ones that we should live close to each other and never meet!!!!!* You write '*tout à vous.*' Oh! you humbug! said I. No! no! it is really too bad. I should like to thank you 9,000 times for all your efforts on my behalf, and to reproach you 20,000 that you came and went as you did. So all is a delusion! friendship, kingdom, empire; all is only a vapour which every breeze wafts into a different form!! Perhaps I may go to Töplitz, but it is not certain. I might take advantage of that opportunity to let the people of Prague hear something—what think you? if *indeed you still think of me at all!* As the affair with Lobkowitz is now also come to a close, we may write *Finis*, though it far from *fine is* for me.

Baron Pasqualati will no doubt soon call on you again; he also has taken much trouble on my account. Yes indeed! it is easy to talk of *justice*, but to obtain it from others is *no easy matter.* In what way can I be of service to you in my own art? Say whether you prefer my celebrating the monologue of a fugitive king, or

* Kauka evidently had been recently in Vienna without visiting Beethoven.

the perjury of a usurper—or the true friends who though near neighbours never saw each other? In the hope of soon hearing from you—for being now so far asunder it is easier to hold intercourse than when nearer!—I remain, with highest esteem,

Your ever devoted friend,

LUDWIG VAN BEETHOVEN.

149.

*To Herr Kauka.*

1815.

My dear and worthy K.,

I have just received from the Syndic Baier in R. the good news that you told him yourself about Prince F. K. As for the rest, you shall be perfectly satisfied.

I take the liberty to ask you again to look after my interests with the Kinsky family, and I subjoin the necessary receipt for this purpose [see No. 144]. Perhaps some other way may be found, though it does not as yet occur to me, by means of which I need not importune you in future. On the 15th October [1815] I was attacked by an inflammatory cold, from the consequences of which I still suffer, and my art likewise; but it is to be hoped that I shall now gradually recover, and at all events be able once more to display the riches of my little realm of sweet sounds. Yet I am very poor in all else—owing to the times? to poverty of spirit? or what???? Farewell! Everything around disposes us to *profound silence*; but this shall not be the case as to the bond of friendship and soul that unites us. I loudly proclaim myself, now as ever,

Your loving friend and admirer,

BEETHOVEN.

### 150.

*To Herr Kauka.*

1815.

My most worthy Friend,

My second letter follows that of yesterday, May 2nd. Pasqualati tells me to-day, after the lapse of a month and six days, that the house of Ballabene is too *high and mighty* to assist me in this matter. I must therefore appeal to your *insignificance* (as I myself do not hesitate to be so mean as to serve other people). My house-rent amounts to 550 florins, and must be paid out of the sum in question.

As soon as the newly engraved pianoforte pieces appear, you shall receive copies, and also of the 'Battle,' &c. &c. Forgive me, forgive me, my generous friend; some other means must be found to forward this affair with due promptitude.

In haste, your friend and admirer,

BEETHOVEN.

## 151.

### To Mr. Salomon,—London.*

Vienna, June 1, 1815.

My good Fellow-countryman,

I always hoped to meet you one day in London, but many obstacles have intervened to prevent the fulfilment of this wish, and as there seems now no chance of such a thing, I hope you will not refuse a request of mine, which is, that you will be so obliging as to apply to some London publisher, and offer him the following works of mine. Grand Trio for piano, violin, and violoncello [Op. 97], 80 ducats. Pianoforte Sonata, with violin accompaniment [Op. 96], 60 ducats. Grand Symphony in A (one of my very best); a short Symphony in F [the 8th]; Quartett for two violins, viola, and violoncello in F minor [Op. 95]; Grand Opera in score, 30 ducats. Cantata with Choruses and Solos ['The Glorious Moment'], 30 ducats. Score of the 'Battle of Vittoria' and 'Wellington's Victory,' 80 ducats; also the pianoforte arrangement of the same, if not already published, which, I am told here, is the case. I have named the prices of some of these works, on a scale which I hold to be suitable for England,

---

* J. P. Salomon was likewise a native of Bonn, and one of the most distinguished violin players of his time. He had been Kapellmeister to Prince Heinrich of Prussia, and then went to London, where he was very active in the introduction of German music. It was through his agency that Beethoven's connection with Birchall, the music publisher, first commenced, to whom a number of his letters are addressed.

but I leave it to you to say what sum should be asked both for these and the others. I hear, indeed, that Cramer [John, whose pianoforte playing was highly estimated by Beethoven] is also a publisher, but my scholar Ries lately wrote to me that Cramer not long since *publicly expressed his disapproval of my works* : I trust from no motive but that of *being of service to art*, and if so I have no right to object to his doing this. If, however, Cramer should wish to possess any of my *pernicious* works, I shall be as well satisfied with him as with any other publisher ; but I reserve the right to give these works to be published here, so that they may appear at the same moment in London and Vienna.

Perhaps you may also be able to point out to me in what way I can recover from the Prince Regent [afterwards George IV.] the expenses of transcribing the 'Battle Symphony' on Wellington's victory at Vittoria to be dedicated to him, for I have long ago given up all hope of receiving anything from that quarter. I have not even been deemed worthy of an answer, whether I am to be authorised to dedicate the work to the Prince Regent; and when at last I propose to publish it here, I am informed that it has already appeared in London. What a fatality for an author ! ! ! While the English and German papers are filled with accounts of the success of the work, as performed at Drury Lane, and that theatre drawing great receipts from it, the author has not one friendly line to show, not even payment for the cost of

copying the work, and is thus deprived of all profit.*
For if it be true that the pianoforte arrangement is
soon to be published by a German publisher, copied
from the London one, then I lose both my fame and
my *honorarium.* The well-known generosity of your
character leads me to hope that you will take some
interest in the matter, and actively exert yourself on
my behalf.

The inferior paper-money of this country is now reduced to one-fifth of its value, and I am paid according
to this scale. After many struggles and considerable
loss, I at length succeeded in obtaining the full value,
but at this moment the old paper-money has again risen
far beyond the fifth part, so that it is evident my salary
becomes for the second time almost *nil,* and there is
no hope of any compensation. My whole income is derived from my works. If I could rely on a good sale in
England, it would doubtless be very beneficial to me.
Pray be assured of my boundless gratitude. I hope
soon, very soon, to hear from you.

I am, with esteem, your sincere friend,

LUDWIG VAN BEETHOVEN.

* Undoubtedly the true reading of these last words, which in the
copy before me are marked as 'difficult to decipher.'

## 152.

### To the Archduke Rudolph.

1815.

Pray forgive my asking Y. R. H. to send me the two Sonatas with violin *obbligato*\* which I caused to be transcribed for Y. R. H. I require them only for a few days, when I will immediately return them.

[K.]

## 153.

### To the Archduke Rudolph.

1815.

I beg you will kindly send me the Sonata in E minor,† as I wish to correct it. On Monday I shall enquire for Y. R. H. in person. *Recent occurrences* ‡ render it indispensable to complete many works of mine about to be engraved as quickly as possible; besides, my health is only partially restored. I earnestly entreat Y. R. H. to desire *some one* to write me a few lines as to the state of your own health. I trust I shall hear a better—nay, the best report of it.

[K.]

\* If by the two Sonatas for the pianoforte with violoncello *obbligato*, Op. 102 is meant, they were composed in July—August 1815, and appeared on Jan. 13th, 1819. The date of the letter appears also to be 1815.

† The letters 152 and 153 speak sometimes expressly of the pianoforte Sonata in E minor, Op. 90, these being engraved or under revision, and sometimes only indicate them. This Sonata, dedicated to Count Lichnowsky, was composed on August 14th, 1844, and published in June 1815.

‡ What 'recent occurrences' Beethoven alludes to, unless indeed his well-known misfortunes as to his salary and guardianship, we cannot discover.

### 154.

### *To the Archduke Rudolph.*

1815.

You must almost think my illness a mere fiction, but that is assuredly not the case. I am obliged always to come home early in the evening. The first time that Y. R. H. was graciously pleased to send for me, I came home immediately afterwards, but feeling much better since then, I made an attempt the evening before last to stay out a little later. If Y. R. H. does not countermand me, I intend to have the honour of waiting on you this evening at five o'clock. I will bring the new Sonata with me, merely for to-day, for it is so soon to be engraved that it is not worth while to have it written out.

[K.]

### 155.

### *To the Archduke Rudolph.*

1815.

I intended to have given you this letter myself, but my personal attendance might possibly be an intrusion, so I take the liberty once more to urge on Y. R. H. the request it contains. I should also be glad if Y. R. H. would send me back my last MS. Sonata, for as I *must* publish it, it would be labour lost to have it transcribed, and I shall soon have the pleasure of presenting it to you engraved. I will call again in a few days. I trust these joyous times may have a happy influence on your precious health.

[K.]

## 156.

*To the Archduke Rudolph.*

Vienna, July 23, 1815.

When you were recently in town, the enclosed Chorus* occurred to me. I hurried home to write it down, but was detained longer in doing so than I at first expected, and thus, to my great sorrow, I missed Y. R. H. The bad custom I have followed from childhood, instantly to write down my first thoughts, otherwise they not unfrequently go astray, has been an injury to me on this occasion. I therefore send Y. R. H. my impeachment and my justification, and trust I may find grace in your eyes. I hope soon to present myself before Y. R. H., and to enquire after a health so precious to us all.

[K.]

## 157.

*To the Archduke Rudolph.*

1815.

It is neither presumption, nor the pretension of advocating anyone's cause, still less from the wish of arrogating to myself the enjoyment of any especial favour with Y. R. H., that induces me to make a suggestion which is in itself very simple. Old Kraft † was with me yesterday; he wished to know if it were

* In 1815 the Chorus of ' Die Meeresstille' was composed by Beethoven. Was this the Chorus which occurred to him ? The style of the letter leaves his meaning quite obscure.

† Old Kraft was a clever violoncello player who had an appointment in Prince Lobkowitz's band, but when the financial crisis occurred in the Prince's affairs he lost his situation, and was obliged to give up his lodging.

possible for him to be lodged in your palace, in return for which he would be at Y. R. H.'s service as often as you please it. He has lived for twenty years in the house of Prince Lobkowitz, and during a great part of that time he received no salary; he is now obliged to vacate his rooms without receiving any compensation whatever. The position of the poor deserving old man is hard, and I should have considered myself equally hard, had I not ventured to lay his case before you. Count Troyer will request an answer from Y. R. H. As the object in view is to brighten the lot of a fellow-creature, pray forgive your, &c. &c.

[K.]

### 158.

*Written in English to Mr. Birchall, Music Publisher, London.*

Mr. Beethoven send word to Mr. Birchall that it is severall days past that he has sent for London Welling-ton's Battel Sinphonie and that Mr. B[irchall] may send for it at Thomas Coutts. Mr. Beethoven wish Mr. B. would make ingrave the sayd Sinphonie so soon as possible and send him word in time the day it will be published that he may prevend in time the Pub-lisher in Vienna.

In regard the 3. Sonata which Mr. Birchall receive afterwerths there is not wanted such a g^t. hurry and

Mr. B. will take the liberty to fixe the day when the are to be published.

Mr. B[irchall] sayd that Mr. Salomon has a good many tings to say concerning the Synphonie in G [? A].

Mr. B[eethoven] with for a answer so soon as possible concerning the days of the publication.

### 159.

#### To Zmeskall.

October 16, 1815.

I only wish to let you know that I am *here*, and not *elsewhere*, and wish in return to hear if you are *elsewhere* or *here*. I should be glad to speak to you for a few minutes when I know that you are at home and alone. *Farewell*—but not *too well*—sublime Commandant Pacha of various mouldering fortresses!!!

In haste, your friend,

BEETHOVEN.

### 160.

#### To the Archduke Rudolph.

Nov. 16, 1815.

Since yesterday afternoon I have been lying in a state of exhaustion owing to my great distress of mind caused by the sudden death of my unhappy brother. It was impossible for me to send an answer to Y. R. H. yesterday, and I trust you will graciously receive my present explanation. I expect, however, certainly to wait on Y. R. H. to-morrow.

[K.]

## 161.

### *To the Messrs. Birchall,—London.*

Vienna, Nov. 22, 1815.

You will herewith receive the pianoforte arrangement of the Symphony in A. 'Wellington's Battle Symphony' and 'Victory at Vittoria' were sent a month since through Herr Neumann, to the care of Messrs. Coutts, so you have no doubt received them long ere this.

In the course of a fortnight you shall have the Trio and Sonata, when you are requested to pay into the hands of Messrs. Coutts the sum of 130 gold ducats. I beg you will make no delay in bringing out these works, and likewise let me know on what day the 'Wellington Symphony' is to appear, so that I may take my measures here accordingly. I am, with esteem,

Your obedient

LUDWIG VAN BEETHOVEN.

## 162.

### *To Ries.*

Vienna, Wednesday, Nov. 22, 1815.

My dear Ries,

I hasten to apprise you that I have to-day forwarded by post the pianoforte arrangement of the Symphony in A, to the care of Messrs Coutts. As the Court is absent, few, indeed almost no couriers go from here; moreover, the post is the safest way. The Symphony ought to be brought out about March; the precise day I will fix myself. So much time has already been lost on this occasion that I could not give an earlier notice of the period of publication. The Trio in [??] and the violin Sonata may be allowed more time, and both will be in London a few weeks hence. I earnestly entreat you, dear Ries, to take charge of these matters, and also to see that I get the money; I require it, and it costs me a good deal before all is sent off.

I have lost 600 florins of my yearly salary; at the time of the *bank notes* there was no loss, but then came the *Einlösungsscheine* [reduced paper-money], which deprives me of these 600 florins, after entailing on me several years of annoyance, and now the total loss of my salary. We are at present arrived at a point when the *Einlösungsscheine* are even lower than the *bank notes* ever were. I pay 1,000 florins of house-rent: you may thus conceive all the misery caused by paper-money.

My poor unhappy brother [Carl v. Beethoven, a cashier in Vienna] is just dead [Nov. 15th, 1815]; he had a bad wife. For some years past he has been suffering from consumption, and from my wish to make his life less irksome I may compute what I gave him at 10,000 florins (*Wiener Währung*). This indeed does not seem much to an Englishman, but it is a great deal for a poor German, or rather Austrian. The unhappy man was latterly much changed, and I must say I lament him from my heart, though I rejoice to think I left nothing undone that could contribute to his comfort.

Tell Mr. Birchall that he is to repay the postage of my letters to you and Mr. Salomon, and also yours to me; he may deduct this from the sum he owes me: I am anxious that those who work for me should lose as little as possible by it. 'Wellington's Victory at Vittoria'* must have arrived long ago through the Messrs. Coutts. Mr. Birchall need not send payment till he is in possession of all the works; only do not delay letting me know when the day is fixed for the publication of the pianoforte arrangement. For to-day, I only further earnestly recommend my affairs to your care; I shall be equally at your service at any time. Farewell, dear Ries.

Your friend,<br>BEETHOVEN.

163.

*To Zmeskall.*

Jan. 1816.

My good Zmeskall,

I was shocked to discover to-day that I had omitted replying to a proposal from the 'Society of Friends to Music in the Austrian States' to write an Oratorio for them.

---

* 'This is also to be the title of the pianoforte arrangement.' (Note by Beethoven.)

The death of my brother two months ago, which, owing to the guardianship of my nephew having devolved on me, has involved me in all sorts of annoyances and perplexities, has caused this delay in my answer. In the meantime, the poem of Herr van Seyfried is already begun, and I purpose shortly to set it to music. I need not tell you how very flattering I consider such a commission, for how could I think otherwise? and I shall endeavour to acquit myself as honourably as my poor talents will admit of.

*With regard to our artistic resources,* when the time for the performance arrives I shall certainly take into consideration those usually at our disposal, without, however, strictly limiting myself to them. I hope I have made myself clearly understood on this point. As I am urged to say what gratuity I require in return, I beg to know whether the Society will consider 400 gold ducats a proper remuneration for such a work? I once more entreat the forgiveness of the Society for the delay in my answer, but I am in some degree relieved by knowing that, at all events, you, my dear friend, have already verbally apprised the Society of my readiness to write a work of the kind.*

Ever, my worthy Z.,<br>Your BEETHOVEN.

* In the 'Fischof'sche Handschrift' we are told:—'The allusion to "our artistic resources" requires some explanation. Herr v. Zmeskall had at that time received instructions to give a hint to the great com-

## 164.

### *To Mdlle. Milder-Hauptmann.**

Vienna, Jan. 6, 1816.

My highly valued Mdlle. Milder, my dear Friend,

I have too long delayed writing to you. How gladly would I personally participate in the enthusiasm you excite at Berlin in ' Fidelio' ! A thousand thanks on my part for having so faithfully adhered to *my* ' Fidelio.' If you will ask Baron de la Motte-Fouqué, in my name, to discover a good subject for an Opera, and one suitable likewise to yourself, you will do a real service both to me and to the German stage; it is also my wish to write it expressly for the *Berlin Theatre,* as no new Opera can ever succeed in being properly given here

poser (who paid little regard to the difficulty of executing his works) that he must absolutely take into consideration the size of the orchestra, which at grand concerts amounted to 700 performers. The Society only stipulated for the exclusive right to the work for one year, and did not purchase the copyright; they undertook the gratuity for the poem also, so they were obliged to consult their pecuniary resources, and informed the composer that they were prepared to give him 200 gold ducats for the use of the work for a year, as they had proposed. Beethoven was quite satisfied, and made no objection whatever ; he received an advance on this sum according to his own wish, the receipt of which he acknowledged in 1819. Beethoven rejected the first poem selected, and desired to have another. The Society left his choice quite free. Herr Bernhard undertook to supply a new one. Beethoven and he consulted together in choosing the subject, but Herr Bernhard, overburdened by other business, could only send the poem bit by bit. Beethoven, however, would not begin till the whole was in his hands.

\* Mdlle. Milder married Hauptmann, a jeweller in Munich, in 1810, travelled in 1812, and was engaged at Berlin in 1816.

under this very penurious direction.    Answer me soon, very soon— quickly, very quickly—as quickly as possible —as quick as lightning—and say whether such a thing is practicable.    Herr Kapellmeister B. praised you up to the skies to me, and he is right; well may he esteem himself happy who has the privilege of enjoying your muse, your genius, and all your splendid endowments and talents;—it is thus I feel.    Be this as it may, those around can only call themselves your fellow-creatures [Nebenmann], whereas I alone have a right to claim the honoured name of captain [*Hauptmann*].

In my secret heart, your true friend and admirer,

BEETHOVEN.

My poor unfortunate brother is dead, which has been the cause of my long silence.    As soon as you have replied to this letter, I will write myself to Baron de la Motte-Fouqué.    No doubt your influence in Berlin will easily obtain for me a commission to write a Grand Opera (in which you shall be especially studied) on favourable terms; but do answer me soon, that I may arrange my other occupations accordingly.

Away with all other false *Hauptmänner* ! [captains].

## 165.

### To Ries.

Vienna, Jan. 20, 1816.

Dear Ries,

The Symphony is to be dedicated to the Empress of Russia. The pianoforte score of the Symphony in A must not, however, appear before June, for the publisher here cannot be ready sooner. Pray, dear Ries, inform Mr. Birchall of this at once. The Sonata with violin accompaniment, which will be sent from here by the next post, can likewise be published in London in May, but the Trio at a later date (it follows by the next post); I will myself name the time for its publication. And now, dear Ries, pray receive my heartfelt thanks for your kindness, and especially for the corrections of the proofs. May Heaven bless you more and more, and promote your progress, in which I take the most sincere interest. My kind regards to your wife. Now as ever,

Your sincere friend,

LUDWIG VAN BEETHOVEN.

## 166.

### To Mr. Birchall,—London.

Vienne, le 3. Febr. den 1816.

Vous receues ci joint

Le grand Trio p. Pf. V. et Vllo. Sonata pour Pf. et Violin—qui form le reste de ce qu'il vous a plus à me

comettre. Je vous prie de vouloir payer la some de 130
Ducats d'Holland come le poste lettre a Mr. Th. Cutts et
Co. de votre ville e de me croire avec toute l'estime et
consideration

votre tres humble Serviteur

LOUIS VAN BEETHOVEN.

167.

*To Czerny.**

My dear Czerny,

Pray give the enclosed to your parents for the
dinners the boy had recently at your house; I positively
will not accept these *gratis*. Moreover, I am very far
from wishing that your lessons should remain without
remuneration—even those already given must be reckoned up and paid for; only I beg you to have a little
patience for a time, as nothing can be *demanded* from
the widow, and I had and still have heavy expenses to
defray;—but I *borrow* from you for the moment only.
The boy is to be with you to-day, and I shall come later.

Your friend,

BEETHOVEN.

---

* Carl Czerny, the celebrated pianist and composer, for whom Beethoven
wrote a testimonial in 1805 (see No. 42). He gave lessons to Beethoven's
nephew in 1815, and naturally protested against any payment, which
gave rise to the expressions on the subject in many of his notes to
Czerny, of which there appear to be a great number.

## 168.

### To Czerny.*

Vienna, Feb. 12, 1816.

Dear Czerny,

I cannot see you to-day, but I will call to-morrow, being desirous to talk to you. I spoke out so bluntly yesterday that I much regretted it afterwards. But you must forgive this on the part of an author, who would have preferred hearing his work as he wrote it, however charmingly you played it. I will, however, *amply* atone for this by the violoncello Sonata.†

Rest assured that I cherish the greatest regard for you as an artist, and I shall always endeavour to prove this.

Your true friend,

BEETHOVEN.

## 169.

### To Ries,—London.

Vienna, Feb. 28, 1816.

. . . For some time past I have been far from well ; the loss of my brother affected both my spirits and my

---

* Czerny, in the 'A. M. Zeitung,' 1845, relates :—' On one occasion (in 1812), at Schuppanzigh's concert, when playing Beethoven's Quintett with wind-instruments, I took the liberty, in my youthful levity, to make many alterations—such as introducing difficulties into the passages, making use of the upper octaves, &c. &c. Beethoven sternly and deservedly reproached me for this, in the presence of Schuppanzigh, Linke, and the other performers.'

† Opera 69, which Czerny (see ' A. M. Zeitung') was to perform with Linke the following week.

works. Salomon's death grieves me much, as he was an excellent man whom I have known from my childhood. You are his executor by will, while I am the guardian of my late poor brother's child. You can scarcely have had as much vexation from Salomon's death as I have had from that of my brother!—but I have the sweet consolation of having rescued a poor innocent child from the hands of an unworthy mother. Farewell, dear Ries; if I can in any way serve you, look on me as

Your true friend,<br>BEETHOVEN.

170.<br>

*To Giannatasio del Rio,— Vienna.*

Feb. 1816.

Sir,

I have great pleasure in saying that at last I intend to-morrow to place under your care the dear pledge entrusted to me. But I must impress on you not to permit any influence on the mother's part to decide when and where she is to see her son. We can, however, discuss all this more minutely to-morrow. . . . You must keep a watchful eye on your servant, for mine was *bribed by her* on one occasion. More as to this verbally, though it is a subject on which I would fain be silent; but the future welfare of the youth you are to train renders this unpleasant communication necessary. I remain, with esteem,

Your faithful servant and friend,<br>BEETHOVEN.

### 171.
### *To G. del Rio.*

1816.

Your estimable lady, Mdme. A. G. [Giannatasio] is politely requested to let the undersigned know as soon as possible (that I may not be obliged to keep it all in my head) how many pairs of stockings, trowsers, shoes, and drawers are required, and how many yards of kerseymere to make a pair of black trowsers for my tall nephew; and for the sake of the 'Castalian Spring' I beg, without any further reminders on my part, that I may receive an answer to this.

As for the Lady Abbess [a nickname for their only daughter], there shall be a conference held on Carl's affair to-night, viz., if things are to continue as they are.

Your well (and ill) born
BEETHOVEN.

### 172.
### *To G. del Rio.*

1816.

I heard yesterday evening, unluckily at too late an hour, that you had something to give me; had it not been for this, I would have called on you. I beg, however, that you will send it, as I have no doubt it is a letter for me from the 'Queen of the Night.' * Although

---

* The 'Queen of the Night' was the name given to Carl's mother by Beethoven. She was a person of great levity of conduct and bad repu-

you gave me permission to fetch Carl twice already, I must ask you to let him come to me when I send for him at eleven o'clock to-morrow, as I wish to take him with me to hear some interesting music. It is also my intention to make him play to me to-morrow, as it is now some time since I heard him. I hope you will urge him to study more closely than usual to-day, that he may in some degree make up for his holiday. I embrace you cordially, and remain,

Yours truly,

LUDWIG VAN BEETHOVEN.

173.

*To G. del Rio.**

1816.

I send you, dear Sir, the cloak, and also a school-book of my Carl's, and request you will make out a list of his clothes and effects, that I may have it copied for myself, being obliged, as his guardian, to look carefully after his property. I intend to call for Carl to-morrow about half-past twelve o'clock to take him to a little concert, and wish him to dine with me afterwards, and shall bring him back myself. With respect to his mother,

tation, and every effort was made by Beethoven to withdraw her son from her influence, on which account he at once removed him from her care, and placed him in this Institution. She consequently appealed to the law against him—the first step in a long course of legal proceedings of the most painful nature.

\* Beethoven's arbitrary authority had been previously sanctioned by a decree of the Court, and the mother deprived of all power over her son.

I desire that *under the pretext* of the boy being *so busy,* you will not let her see him; no man on earth can know or judge of this matter better than myself, and by any other line of conduct all my well-matured plans for the welfare of the child might be materially injured. I will myself discuss with you when the mother is henceforth to have access to Carl, for I am anxious on every account to prevent the occurrence of yesterday ever being repeated. I take all the responsibility on myself; indeed, so far as I am concerned, the Court conferred on me full powers, and the authority at once to counteract anything adverse to the welfare of the boy. If they could have looked on her in the light of an estimable mother, they assuredly would not have excluded her from the guardianship of her child. Whatever she may think fit to assert, nothing has been done in a clandestine manner against her. There was but one voice in the whole council on the subject. I hope to have no further trouble in this matter, for the burden is already heavy enough.

From a conversation I had yesterday with Adlersburg [his lawyer], it would appear that a long time must yet elapse before the Court can decide what really belongs to the child. In addition to all these anxieties am I also to endure a persecution such as I have recently experienced, and from which I thought I *was entirely rescued by your Institution?* Farewell!

I am, with esteem, your obedient
L. v. BEETHOVEN.

174.

*To Ferdinand Ries,—London.*

Vienna, March 8, 1816.

My answer has been too long delayed; but I was ill, and had a great press of business. Not a single farthing is yet come of the ten gold ducats, and I now almost begin to think that the English are only liberal when in foreign countries. It is the same with the Prince Regent, who has not even sent me the cost of copying my ' Battle Symphony,' nor one verbal or written expression of thanks. My whole income consists of 3,400 florins, in paper-money. I pay 1,100 for house-rent, and 900 to my servant and his wife, so you may reckon for yourself what remains. Besides this, the entire maintenance of my young nephew devolves on me. At present he is at school, which costs 1,100 florins, and is by no means a good one, so that I must arrange a proper household and have him with me. How much money must be made to live at all here ! and yet there seems no end to it—because !—because ! —because !—but you know well what I mean.

Some commissions from the Philharmonic would be very acceptable to me, besides the concert. Now let me say that my dear scholar Ries must set to work and dedicate something valuable to me, to which his master may respond, and repay him in his own coin. How can I send you my portrait ? My kind regards to your wife.

I, alas! have none. One alone I wished to possess, but
never shall I call her mine!* This, however, has not
made me a woman-hater.

Your true friend,

BEETHOVEN.

175.

*To F. Ries.*

Vienna, April 3, 1816.

Neate† is no doubt in London by this time. He
took several of my works with him, and promised to
do the best he could for me.

The Archduke Rudolph [Beethoven's pupil. See

---

* See the statement of Fräulein del Rio in the 'Grenzboten.' We read:
—' My father's idea was that marriage alone could remedy the sad condition of Beethoven's household matters, so he asked him whether he
knew anyone, &c. &c. Our long-existing presentiment was then realised.'
His love was unfortunate. Five years ago he had become acquainted with
a person with whom he would have esteemed it the highest felicity of
his life to have entered into closer ties; but it was vain to think of it,
being almost an impossibility! a chimera! and yet his feelings remained the same as the very first day he had seen her! He added, 'that
never before had he found such harmony! but no declaration had ever
been made, not being able to prevail on himself to do so.' This conversation took place in Sept., 1816, at Helenenthal, in Baden, and the
person to whom he alluded was undoubtedly Marie L. Pachler-Koschak
in Gratz. (See No. 80.)

† Charles Neate, a London artist, as Schindler styles him in his
'Biography' (ii. 254), was on several different occasions for some time
resident in Vienna, and very intimate with Beethoven, whom he tried
to persuade to come to London. He also was of great service in pro-
moting the sale of his works. A number of Neate's letters preserved
in the Berlin State Library testify his faithful and active devotion, and
attachment to the master.

No. 70] also plays your works with me, my dear Ries ;
of these ' *Il Sogno* ' especially pleased us.   Farewell !
Remember me to your charming wife, and to any fair
English ladies who care to receive my greetings.

Your true friend,<br>
BEETHOVEN.

### 176.

### *Power of Attorney.*

Vienna, May 2, 1816.

I authorise Herr v. Kauka, Doctor of Laws in the
kingdom of Bohemia, relying on his friendship, to obtain
for me the receipt  of 600 florins W. W., payable at the
treasury of Prince Kinsky, from the house of Ballabene
in Prague, and after having drawn the money to transmit the same to me as soon as possible.

Witness my hand and seal.<br>
LUDWIG VAN BEETHOVEN.

### 177.

### *To F. Ries.*

Vienna, June 11, 1816.

My dear Ries,

I regret much to put you to the expense of postage
on my account ; gladly as I assist and serve everyone, I
am always unwilling myself to have recourse to others.
I have as yet seen nothing of the ten ducats, whence I
draw the inference that in England, just as with us,
there are idle talkers who prove false to their word. I do
not at all blame you in this matter.   I have not heard

a syllable from Neate, so I do wish you would ask him
whether he has disposed of the F minor Concerto. I am
almost ashamed to allude to the other works I entrusted
to him, and equally so of myself, for having given them
to him so confidingly, devoid of all conditions save
those suggested by his own friendship and zeal for my
interests.

A translation has been sent to me of an article in
the 'Morning Chronicle' on the performance of the
Symphony.   Probably it will be the same as to this and
all the other works Neate took with him as with the
'Battle Symphony;' the only profit I shall derive will
be reading a notice of their performance in the newspapers.

178.

*To G. del Rio.*

1816.

My worthy G.,

I beg you will send Carl to me with the bearer of
this letter, otherwise I shall not be able to see him all
day, which would be contrary to his own interest, as my
influence seems to be required ; in the same view, I beg
you will give him a few lines with a report of his conduct, so that I may enter at once on any point where
improvement is necessary.

I am going to the country to-day, and shall not return
till rather late at night ; being always unwilling to
infringe your rules, I beg you will send some night-

things with Carl, so that if we return too late to bring him to you to-day, I can keep him all night, and take him back to you myself early next morning.

In haste, always yours,<br>L. v. BEETHOVEN.

179.

*To G. del Rio.*

1816.

I must apologise to you, my good friend, for Carl having come home at so late an hour. We were obliged to wait for a person who arrived so late that it detained us, but I will not soon repeat this breach of your rules. As to Carl's mother, I have now decided that your wish not to see her again in your house shall be acceded to. This course is far more safe and judicious for our dear Carl, experience having taught me that every visit from his mother leaves a root of bitterness in the boy's heart, which may injure, but never can benefit him. I shall strive to arrange occasional meetings at my house, which is likely to result in everything being entirely broken off with her. As we thoroughly agree on the subject of Carl's mother, we can mutually decide on the mode of his education.

Your true friend,<br>BEETHOVEN.

## 180.

### *To the Archduke Rudolph.*

Vienna, July 11, 1816.

Your kindness towards me induces me to hope that you will not attribute to any *selfish* design on my part the somewhat audacious (though only as to the surprise) dedication annexed. The work * was written for Y. R. H., or rather, it owes its existence to you, and this the world (the musical world) ought to know. I shall soon have the honour of waiting on Y. R. H. in Baden. Notwithstanding all the efforts of my physician, who will not allow me to leave this, the weakness in my chest is no better, though my general health is improved. I hope to hear all that is cheering of your own health, about which I am always so much interested.

[K.]

## 181.

### *Written in English to Mr. Birchall.*

1816.

Received March 1816 of Mr. Robert Birchall—Music-seller 133 New Bond Street London—the sum of One Hundred and thirty Gold Dutch Ducats, value in

---

* Does Beethoven here allude to the dedication of the Sonata for pianoforte and violin in G major, Op. 96, which, though sold to a publisher in April 1815, was designated as quite new in the 'Allgemeine Zeitung' on July 29, 1816?

English Currency Sixty Five Pounds for all my Copy-right and Interest, present and future, vested or contingent, or otherwise within the United kingdom of Great Britain and Ireland in the four following Compositions or Pieces of Music composed or arranged by me, viz.

1st. A Grand Battle Sinfonia, descriptive of the Battle and Victory at Vittoria, adopted for the Pianoforte and dedicated to His Royal Highness the Prince Regent —40 Ducats.

2nd. A Grand Symphony in the key of A, adapted to the Pianoforte and dedicated to —

3d. A Grand Trio for the Pianoforte, Violon and Violoncello in the key of B.

4th. A Sonata for the Pianoforte with an Accompaniment for the Violin in the key of G. dedicated to —

And, in consideration of such payment I hereby for myself, my Executors and Administrators promise and engage to execute a proper Anignment thereof to him, his Executors and Administrators or Anignees at his or their Request and Costs, as he or they shall direct.— And I likewise promise and engage as above, that nome of the above shall be published in any foreign Country, before the time and day fixed and agreed on for such Publication between R. Birchall and myself shall arrive.

L. van Beethoven.

### 182.

*Written in French to Mr. Birchall,—London.*

Vienne 22. Juilliet 1816.

Monsieur.

J'ai reçu la déclaration de proprieté de mes Oeuvres entierement cedé a Vous pour y adjoindre ma Signature. Je suis tout a fait disposer a seconder vos voeux si tôt, que cette affaire sera entierement en ordre, en egard de la petite somme de 10 ♯ d'or la quelle me vient encore pour le fieux de la Copieture de poste de lettre etc. comme j'avois l'honneur de vous expliquier dans une note detaillé sur ses objectes. Je vous invite donc Monsieur de bien vouloir me remettre ces petits objects, pour me mettre dans l'état de pouvoir vous envoyer le Document susdit. Agrées Monsieur l'assurance de l'estime la plus parfait avec la quelle j'ai l'honneur de me dire

LOUIS VAN BEETHOVEN.

| | | |
|---|---|---|
| Copying . . . . . | 1. | 10. 0. |
| Postage to Amsterdam | 1. | 0. 0. |
| —— Trio . . . | 2. | 10. — |
| | £5. | 0. 0. |

### 183.

*To G. del Rio.*

July 28, 1816.

My good Friend,

Various circumstances compel me to take charge of Carl myself; with this view permit me to enclose

you the amount due at the approaching quarter, at the
expiry of which Carl is to leave you. Do not, I beg,
ascribe this to anything derogatory either to yourself
or to your respected Institution, but to other pressing
motives connected with Carl's welfare. It is only an
experiment, and when it is actually carried out I shall
beg you to fortify me by your advice, and also to permit
Carl sometimes to visit your Institution. I shall always
feel the most sincere gratitude to you, and never can
forget your solicitude, and the kind care of your excellent wife, which has fully equalled that of the best of
mothers. I would send you at least four times the sum
I now do, if my position admitted of it, but at all events
I shall avail myself at a future and, I hope, a brighter
day, of every opportunity to acknowledge and to do
justice to the foundation *you* have laid for the moral
and physical good of my Carl. With regard to the
' Queen of the Night,' our system must continue the
same, and as Carl is about to undergo an operation in
your house which will cause him to feel indisposed, and
consequently make him irritable and susceptible, you
must be more careful than ever to prevent her having
access to him, otherwise she might easily contrive to
revive all those impressions in his mind which we are
so anxious to avoid. What confidence can be placed in
any promised reform on her part, the impertinent scrawl
I enclose will best prove [in reference, no doubt, to an
enclosed note]. I send it merely to show you how fully

I am justified in the precautions I have already adopted with regard to her. On this occasion, however, I did not answer like a Sarastro, but like a Sultan. I would gladly spare you the anxiety of the operation on Carl, but as it must take place in your house, I beg you will inform me of the outlay caused by the affair, and the expenses consequent on it, which I will thankfully repay. Now farewell! Say all that is kind from me to your dear children and your excellent wife, to whose continued care I commend my Carl. I leave Vienna to-morrow at 5 o'clock A.M., but shall frequently come in from Baden.

Ever, with sincere esteem, your

L. v. BEETHOVEN.

### 184.

#### To G. del Rio.

Mdme. A. G. is requested to order several pairs of good linen drawers for Carl. I entrust Carl to her kindness, and entirely rely on her motherly care.

### 185.

#### To Zmeskall.

Baden, September 5, 1816.

Dear Z.,

I dont know whether you received a note that I recently left on the threshold of your door, for the time was too short to enable me to see you. I must therefore

repeat my request about another servant, as the conduct
of my present one is such that I cannot possibly keep
him.* He was engaged on the 25th of April, so on the
25th of September he will have been five months with me,
and he received 50 florins on account. The money for
his boots will be reckoned from the third month (in my
service), and from that time at the rate of 40 florins per
annum, his livery also from the third month. From
the very first I resolved not to keep him, but delayed
discharging him, as I wished to get back the value of
my florins. In the meantime, if I can procure another,
I will let this one leave my service on the 15th of the
month, and also give him 20 florins for boot money, and
5 florins a month for livery (both reckoned from the
third month), making altogether 35 florins. I ought
therefore still to receive 15 florins, but these I am
willing to give up; in this way I shall at all events receive some equivalent for my 50 florins. If you can
find a suitable person, I will give him 2 florins a day
while I am in Baden, and if he knows how to cook he
can use my firewood in the kitchen. (I have a kitchen,
though I do not cook in it.) If not, I will add a few
kreuzers to his wages. As soon as I am settled in
Vienna, he shall have 40 florins a month, and board and
livery as usual, reckoned from the third month in my
service, like other servants. It would be a good thing

---

* During a quarrel, the servant scratched Beethoven's face.

if he understood a little tailoring. So now you have my proposals, and I beg for an answer by the 10th of this month at the latest, that I may discharge my present servant on the 2nd, with the usual fortnight's warning ; otherwise I shall be obliged to keep him for another month, and every moment I wish to get rid of him. As for the new one, you know pretty well what I require—*good, steady conduct,* a *good character,* and *not to be of a bloodthirsty nature,* that I may feel my life to be safe, as, for the sake of various scamps in this world, I should like to live a little longer. By the 10th, therefore, I shall expect to hear from you on this affair. If you don't run restive, I will soon send you my treatise on the four violoncello strings, very profoundly handled ; the first chapter devoted exclusively to entrails in general, the second to catgut in particular. I need scarcely give you any further warnings, as you seem to be quite on your guard against wounds inflicted before certain fortresses. The most *profound peace* everywhere prevails !!! Farewell, my good *Zmeskäll-chen!* I am, as ever, *un povero musico* and your friend,

BEETHOVEN.

N.B.—I shall probably only require my new servant for some months, as, for the sake of my Carl, I must shortly engage a housekeeper.

## 186.

### To Herr Kauka.

Baden, Sept. 6, 1816.

My worthy K.,

I send you herewith the receipt according to your request, and beg that you will kindly arrange that I should have the money by the 1st October, and without any deduction, which has hitherto been the case; I also particularly beg *you will not assign the money to Baron P.* (I will tell you why when we meet; for the present let this remain between ourselves). Send it either direct to myself, or, if it must come through another person, do not let it be Baron P. It would be best for the future, as the house-rent is paid here for the great house belonging to Kinsky, that my money should be paid at the same time. This is only my own idea. The Terzett you heard of will soon be engraved, which is infinitely preferable to all written music; you shall therefore receive an engraved copy, and likewise some more of my unruly offspring. In the meantime I beg that you will see only what is truly good in them, and look with an indulgent eye on the human frailties of these poor innocents. Besides, I am full of cares, being in reality father to my late brother's child; indeed I might have ushered into the world a second part of the *Flauto Magico*, having also been brought into contact with a ' Queen of the Night.' I embrace you from my heart, and hope soon in so far to succeed that you may owe some thanks to my muse. My dèar, worthy Kauka, I ever am your truly attached friend,

BEETHOVEN.

### 187.

*Query?*

What would be the result were I to leave this, and indeed the kingdom of Austria altogether? Would the life-certificate, if signed by the authorities of a non-Austrian place, still be valid?

*A tergo.*

I beg you will let me know the postage all my letters have cost you.

### 188.

*To G. del Rio.*

Sunday, September 22, 1816.

Certain things can never be fully expressed. Of this nature are my feelings, and especially my gratitude, on hearing the details of the operation on Carl from you. You will excuse my attempting even remotely to shape these into words. I feel certain, however, that you will not decline the tribute I gladly pay you;—but I say no more. You can easily imagine my anxiety to hear how my dear son is going on: do not omit to give me your exact address, that I may write to you direct. After you left this I wrote to Bernhard [Bernard], to make enquiries at your house, but have not yet got an answer; so possibly you may have thought me a kind of half-reckless barbarian, as no doubt Herr B. has neglected to call on you, as well as to write to me. I can have no uneasiness about Carl when your admirable wife is with him—that is quite out of the question. You can well understand how much it grieves me not to be able to take part in the sufferings of my Carl, and that I at least wish to hear frequently of his progress. As I have renounced such an unfeeling, unsympathising friend as Herr B. [Bernard], I must have recourse to your friendship and complaisance on this point also, and shall hope soon to receive a few lines from you. I beg to send my best regards and a thousand thanks to your admirable wife.

In haste,

Your Beethoven.

I wish you to express to Smetana [the surgeon] my esteem and high consideration.

189.

To G. del Rio.

If you do not object, I beg you will allow Carl to come to me with the bearer of this. I forgot, in my haste, to say that all the love and goodness which Mdme. A. G. [Giannatasio] showed my Carl during his illness are inscribed in the list of my obligations, and I hope one day to show that they are ever present in my mind. Perhaps I may see you to-day with Carl.

In haste, your sincere friend,

L. v. BEETHOVEN.

## 190.

### To Wegeler.

I take the opportunity through J. Simrock to remind you of myself. I hope you received the engraving of me [by Letronne], and likewise the Bohemian glass. When I next make a pilgrimage through Bohemia you shall have something more of the same kind. Farewell! You are a husband and a father; so am I, but without a wife. My love to your dear ones—to *our* dear ones.

Your friend,

L. v. BEETHOVEN.

## 191.

### Written in English to Mr. Birchall, Music Seller, London.

Vienna, 1. Oct. 1816.

My Dear Sir,

I have duly received the £5 and thought previously you would non increase the number of Englishmen neglecting their word and honor, as I had the misfortune of meeting with two of this sort. In replic to the other topics of your favor, I have no objection to write variations according to your plan, and I hope you will not

find £30 too much, the Acompaniment will be a Flute
or Violon or a Violoncello; you'll either decide it when
you send me the approbation of the price, or you'll leave
it to me.    I expect to receive the songs or poetry—the
sooner the better, and you'll favor me also with the probable number of Works of Variations you are inclined
to receive of me.    The Sonata in G with the accompan^t.
of a Violin to his Imperial Highnesse Archduke Rodolph
of Austria—it is Op^a. 96.    The Trio in B^b is dedicated
to the same and is Op. 97.    The Piano arrangement of
the Symphony in A is dedicated to the Empress of the
Russians—meaning the Wife of the Emp^r. Alexander—
Op. 98.

Concerning the expences of copying and packing it is
not possible to fix him before hand, they are at any rate
not considerable, and you'll please to consider that you
have to deal with a man of honor, who will not charge
one 6^p. more than he is charged for himself.    Messrs.
Fries & Co. will account with Messrs. Coutts & Co.—
The postage may be lessened as I have been told.    I
offer you of my Works the following new ones.    A Grand
Sonata for the Pianoforte alone £40.    A Trio for the
Piano with accomp^t. of Violin and Violoncell for £50.
It is possible that somebody will offer you other works
of mine to purchase, for ex. the score of the Grand Symphony in A.—With regard to the arrangement of this
Symphony for the Piano I beg you not to forget that you
are not to publish it until I have appointed the day of

its publication here in Vienna. This cannot be otherwise without making myself guilty of a dishonorable act— but the Sonata with the Violin and the Trio in B fl. may be published without any delay.

With all the *new works*, which you will have of me or which I offer you, it rests with you to name the day of their publication at your own choise: I entreat you to honor me as soon as possible with an answer having many ordres for compositions and that you may not be delayed. My adress or direction is

Monsieur Louis van Beethoven

No. 1055 & 1056 Sailerstette 3ᵈ· Stock. Vienna.

You may send your letter, if you please, direct to your most humble servant

LUDWIG VAN BEETHOVEN.

### 192.

#### *To Zmeskall.*

Oct. 24, 1816.

Well born, and yet evil born! (as we all are!)

We are in Baden to-day, and intend to bring the celebrated naturalist Ribini a collection of dead leaves. To-morrow we purpose paying you not only a *visit* but a *visitation.*

Your devoted

LUDWIG VAN BEETHOVEN.

## 193.

### *To the Archduke Rudolph.*

November, 1816.*

I have been again much worse, so that I can only
venture to go out a little in the daytime; I am, however,
getting better, and hope now to have the honour of
waiting on Y. R. H. three times a week.    Meanwhile,
I have many and great cares in these terrible times
(which surpass anything we have ever experienced), and
which are further augmented by having become the
father since last November of a poor orphan.    All this
tends to retard my entire restoration to health.    I wish
Y. R. H. all imaginable good and happiness, and beg
you will graciously receive and not misinterpret

Your, &c. &c.

[K.]

## 194.

### *To Freiherr von Schweiger.*

Best!

Most amiable !

First and foremost *Turner Meister* of Europe !

The bearer of this is a poor devil! (like many
another ! ! !).    You could assist him by asking your
gracious master whether he is disposed to purchase one
of his small but neat pianos.    I also beg you will recommend him to any of the Chamberlains or Adjutants

* A year after Carl von Beethoven's death (November 15, 1815).

of the Archduke Carl, to see whether it is possible that H. R. H. would buy one of these instruments for his Duchess. We therefore request an introduction from the illustrious *Turner Meister* for this poor devil * to the Chamberlains and Adjutants of the household.

Likewise

1

poor devil,

[K.]                         L. v. BEETHOVEN.

195.

*To G. del Rio.*

Nov. 16, 1816.

My dear Friend,

My household seems about to make shipwreck, or something very like it. You know that I was duped into taking this house on false pretexts; besides, my health does not seem likely to improve in a hurry. To engage a tutor under such circumstances, whose character and whose very exterior even are unknown to me, and thus to entrust my Carl's education to haphazard, is quite out of the question, no matter how great the sacrifices which I shall be again called on to make. I beg you, therefore, to keep Carl for the ensuing quarter, commencing on the 9th. I will in so far comply with your proposal as to the cultivation of the science of music, that Carl may come to me two or three times a week, leaving you at six o'clock in the

---

* A name cannot now be found for the 'poor devil.'

evening and staying with me till the following morning, when he can return to you by eight o'clock. It would be too fatiguing for Carl to come every day, and indeed too great an effort and tie for me likewise, as the lessons must be given at the same fixed hour.

During this quarter we can discuss more minutely the most suitable plan for Carl, taking into consideration both his interests and my own. I must, alas! mention my own also in these times, which are daily getting worse. If your garden residence had agreed with my health, everything might have been easily adjusted. With regard to my debt to you for the present quarter, I beg you will be so obliging as to call on me, that I may discharge it; the bearer of this has the good fortune to be endowed by Providence with a vast amount of stupidity, which I by no means grudge him the benefit of, provided others do not suffer by it. As to the remaining expenses incurred for Carl, either during his illness or connected with it, I must, for a few days only, request your indulgence, having great calls on me at present from all quarters. I wish also to know what fee I ought to give Smetana for the successful operation he performed; were I rich, or not in the same sad position in which all are who have linked their fate to this country (always excepting *Austrian usurers*), I would make no enquiries on the subject; and I only wish you to give me a rough estimate of the proper fee. Farewell! I cordially embrace you, and shall always look on you as a friend of mine and of Carl's.

I am, with esteem, your

L. v. BEETHOVEN.

196.

*To G. del Rio.*

Though I would gladly spare you all needless disagreeable trouble, I cannot, unluckily, do so on this occasion. Yesterday, in searching for some papers, I found this pile, which has been sent to me respecting Carl. I do not quite understand them, and you would oblige me much by employing some one to make out a regular statement of all your outlay for Carl, so that I may send for it to-morrow. I hope you did not misunderstand me when I yesterday alluded to *magnanimity*, which certainly was not meant for you, but solely for the 'Queen of the Night,' who is never weary of hoisting the sails of her vindictiveness against me, so on this account I require vouchers, more for the satisfaction of others than for her sake (as I never will submit to render her any account of my actions). No stamp is required, and the sum alone for each quarter need be specified, for I believe most of the accounts are forthcoming, so all you have to do is to append them to your *prospectus* the conclusion illegible].

L. v. BEETHOVEN.

## 197.

### To G. del Rio.

Nov. 14, 1816.

My good Friend,

I beg you will allow Carl to come to me to-morrow, as it is the anniversary of his father's death [Nov. 15th], and we wish to visit his grave together. I shall probably come to fetch him between twelve and one o'clock. I wish to know the effect of my treatment of Carl, after your recent complaints. In the meantime, it touched me exceedingly to find him so susceptible as to his honour. Before we left your house I gave him some hints on his want of industry, and while walking together in a graver mood than usual, he pressed my hand vehemently, but met with no response from me. At dinner he scarcely eat anything, and said that he felt very melancholy, the cause of which I could not extract from him. At last, in the course of our walk, he owned that *he was vexed because he had not been so industrious as usual.* I said what I ought on the subject, but in a kinder manner than before. This, however, proves a certain delicacy of feeling, and such *traits* lead me to augur all that is good. If I cannot come to you to-morrow, I hope you will let me know by a few lines the result of my conference with Carl.

I once more beg you to let me have the account due for the last quarter. I thought that you had misunderstood my letter, or even worse than that. I warmly commend my poor orphan to your good heart, and, with kind regards to all, I remain

Your friend,

L. v. BEETHOVEN.

198.

*To G. del Rio.*

My good Friend,

Pray forgive me for having allowed the enclosed sum to be ready for you during the last twelve days or more, and not having sent it. I have been very much occupied, and am only beginning to recover, though indeed the word *recovery* has not yet been pronounced.

In haste, with much esteem, ever yours,

L. v. BEETHOVEN.

199.

*To Herr Tschischka.*

Sir,

It is certainly of some moment to me *not to appear in a false light,* which must account for the accompanying statement being so prolix. As to the future system of education, I can at all events congratulate myself on having done all that I could possibly effect at present *for the best,* and trust *that the future may be in accordance with it.* But if the welfare of my nephew demands a *change,* I shall be the first not only to propose such a step, but *to carry it out.* I am no self-interested guardian, but I wish to establish a new monument to my name through my nephew. I *have no need of my nephew*, but he has need of me. Idle talk and calumnies are beneath the dignity of a man with proper self-respect, and what can be said when these extend even to the subject of linen!!! This might cause me great annoyance, *but a just man ought to be able to bear injustice* without in the *most remote degree* deviating from the path of *right*. In this conviction I will stand fast, and nothing shall make me flinch. To deprive me of my nephew would indeed entail a heavy responsibility. As a matter of *policy* as well as of morality, such a step would be productive of evil results to my nephew. *I urgently recommend his interests to you.* As for me, *my actions* for *his* benefit (not for my *own*) must speak for me.

I remain, with esteem,

Your obedient

BEETHOVEN.

Being very busy, and rather indisposed, I must claim your indulgence for the writing of the memorial.

200.

*Written in English to Mr. Birchall,—London.*

Vienna 14. December 1816—1055 Sailerstette.

Dear Sir,

I give you my word of honor that I have signed and delivered the recept to the home Fries and Co. some

day last August, who as they say have transmitted it
to Messrs. Coutts and Co. where you'll have the goodness to apply. Some error might have taken place that
instead of Mrssrs. C. sending it to you they have been
directed to keep it till fetched. Excuse this irregu-
larity, but it is not my fault, nor had I ever the idea of
witholding it from the circumstance of the £5 not being
included. Should the recept not come forth as Messrs.
C., I am ready to sign any other, and you shall have
it directly with return of post.

If you find Variations—in my style—too dear at £30,
I will abate for the sake of your friendship one third—
and you have the offer of such Variations as fixed in
our former lettres for £20 each Air.

Please to publish the Symphony in A immediately—
as well as the Sonata—and the Trio—they being ready
here. The Grand Opera Fidelio is my work. The arrangement for the Pianoforte has been published here
under my care, but the score of the Opera itself is not
yet published. I have given a copy of the score to
Mr. Neate under the seal of friendship and whom I
shall direct to treat for my account in case an offer
should present.

I anxiously hope your health is improving, give me
leave to subscrive myself

Dear Sir

Your very obedient Serv.

LUDWIG VAN BEETHOVEN.

## 201.

### *To Zmeskall.*

Dec. 16, 1816.

With this, dear Zmeskall, you will receive my friendly dedication [a stringed Quartett, Op. 95], which may, I hope, serve as a pleasant memorial of our long enduring friendship here; pray accept it as a proof of my esteem, and not merely as the extreme end of a thread long since spun out (for you are one of my earliest friends in Vienna).

Farewell! Beware of mouldering fortresses! for an attack on them will be more trying than on those in a better state of preservation! As ever,

Your friend,

BEETHOVEN.

N.B.—When you have a moment's leisure, let me know the probable cost of a livery, without linen, but including hat and boots. Strange changes have come to pass in my house. The man is off to the devil, I am thankful to say, whereas his wife seems the more resolved to take root here.

## 202.

### *To Frau von Streicher—née Stein.*

Dec. 28, 1816.

N—— ought to have given you the New Year's tickets yesterday, but it seems she did not do so. The day before I was occupied with Maelzel, whose business was pressing, as he leaves this so soon, otherwise you may be sure that I would have hurried up again to see you. Your dear kind daughter was with me yesterday, but I scarcely ever remember being so ill; my *precious servants* were occupied from seven o'clock till ten at night in trying to heat the stove. The bitter cold, particularly in my room, caused me a chill, and the whole of yesterday I could scarcely move a limb. All day I was coughing, and had the most severe headache I ever had in my life, so by six o'clock in the evening I was obliged to go to bed, where I still am, though feeling somewhat better. Your brother dined with me yesterday, and has shown me great kindness. You are aware that on the same day, the 27th of December, I discharged B. [Baberl]. I cannot endure either of these vile creatures; I wonder if Nany will behave rather better from the departure of her colleague? I doubt it —but in that case I shall send her *packing* without any ceremony. She is too uneducated for a housekeeper, indeed quite a *beast*; but the other, in spite of her pretty face, is even *lower than the beasts*. As the New Year draws near, I think five florins will be enough for Nany; I have not paid her the charge for *making her spencer*, on account of her *bad behaviour to you*. The other certainly *deserves no New Year's gift*; besides, she has nine florins of mine on hand, and when she leaves I don't expect to receive more than four or five florins of

that sum. I wish to have *your opinion about all this.*
Pray accept my best wishes for your welfare, which are
offered in all sincerity. I am your debtor in so many
ways, that I really often feel quite ashamed. Farewell;
I trust I may always retain your friendship.

Now, as ever, your friend,

L. v. BEETHOVEN.

203.

*To Frau von Streicher.*

I thank you for the interest you take in me. I am
rather better, though to-day again I have been obliged
to endure a great deal from Nany; but I shied half a
dozen books at her head by way of a New Year's gift.
We have stripped off the leaves (by sending off Baberl)
and lopped off the branches, but we must extirpate the
*roots*, till nothing is left but the actual soil.

204.

*To Frau von Streicher.*

Nany is not strictly *honest,* and an odiously stupid
*animal* into the bargain. Such people must be managed
not by *love* but by *fear.* I now see this clearly. Her
account-book alone cannot show you everything clearly;
you must often drop in unexpectedly at dinner-time,
like an avenging angel, to see with your own eyes *what*

we actually have.   I never dine at home now, *unless*
I have some friend as my guest, for I have no wish to
pay as much for one person as would serve for four.
I shall *now soon* have my dear son Carl with me, so
economy is more necessary than ever.   I cannot prevail
on myself to go to you : I know you will forgive this.
I am very sensitive, and not used to such things, so the
less ought I to expose myself to them.   In addition to
twelve kreuzers for bread, Nany has a roll of white bread
every morning.   Is this usual ?— and it is the same with
the cook.   A daily roll for breakfast comes to eighteen
florins a year.   *Farewell,* and *work well* for me.   Mdlle.
Nany is wonderfully changed for the better since I sent
the half-dozen books at her head.   Probably they chanced
to come in collision with her *dull brain* or her *bad
heart* ; at all events, she now plays the part of a penitent swindler ! ! !

In haste, yours,

BEETHOVEN.

205.

*To Frau von Streicher.*

Nany yesterday took me to task in the vulgar manner
usual with people of her *low class,* about my complaining to you, so she evidently knew that I had written
to you on the subject.   All the devilry began again
yesterday morning, but I made short work of it by
throwing the heavy arm-chair beside my bed at B.'s

head, which procured me peace for the rest of the day. They always take their revenge on me when I write to you, or when they discover any communication between us.

I do thank Heaven that I everywhere find men who interest themselves in me; one of the *most distinguished Professors* in this University has in the kindest manner undertaken *all that concerns Carl's education.* If you happen to meet any of the Giannatasios at Czerny's, you had better *know nothing of what is going on about Carl,* and say that it is *contrary* to my *usual habit to disclose my plans, as when a project is told to others it is no longer exclusively your own.* They would like to interfere in the matter, and I do not choose that these *commonplace people should do so, both for* my *own sake and Carl's.* Over their portico is inscribed, in golden letters, 'Educational Institution,' whereas ' *Non*-Educational Institution' would be more appropriate.

As for the servants, there is only *one voice* about their immorality, to which *all* the other annoyances here may be ascribed.

Pray receive my benediction in place of that of the Klosterneuburgers.*

In haste, your friend,<br>BEETHOVEN.

---

* Frau von Streicher was at that time in Klosterneuburg.

## 206.

### *To Frau von Streicher.*

Judgment was executed to-day on the notorious criminal! She bore it nearly in the same spirit as Cæsar did Brutus' dagger, except that in the former case truth formed the basis, while in hers only wicked malice. The kitchenmaid seems more handy than the former *ill-conducted beauty*; she no longer shows herself—a sign that she does not expect a *good character* from me, though I really had some thoughts of giving her one. The kitchenmaid at first made rather a wry face about carrying wood, &c.

## 207.

### *To the Archduke Rudolph.*

Last day of December, 1816.

I have been again obliged to keep my room ever since the Burgher concert,* and some time must no doubt elapse before I shall be able to dismiss all precautions as to my health. The year is about to close; and with this new year my warmest wishes are renewed for the welfare of Y. R. H.; but indeed these have neither beginning nor end with me, for every day I cherish the same aspirations for Y. R. H. If I may venture to add a wish for myself to the foregoing, it is, that I may daily thrive and prosper more in Y. R. H.'s good graces. The

---

* Beethoven directed his A major Symphony in the Burgher concert in the Royal Redoutensaal on the 25th December, 1816.

master will always strive not to be unworthy of the favour of his illustrious master and pupil.

[K.]

### 208.

#### *To G. del Rio.*

. . . As to his mother, she urgently requested to see Carl in my house. You have sometimes seen me tempted to place more confidence in her, and my feelings would lead me to guard against harshness towards her, especially as it is not in her power to injure Carl. But you may well imagine that to one usually so independent of others, the annoyances to which I am exposed through Carl are often utterly insupportable, and above all with regard to his mother; I am only too glad to hear nothing of her, which is the cause of my avoiding her name. With respect to Carl, I beg you will enforce the strictest discipline on him, and if he refuses to obey your orders or to do his duty, I trust you will at once *punish* him. Treat him as if he were your own child rather than a *mere pupil*, for I already told you that during his father's lifetime he only submitted to the discipline of blows—which was a bad system: still, such was the fact, and we must not forget it.

If you do not see much of me, pray ascribe it solely to the little inclination I have for society, which is sometimes more developed and sometimes less; and this you might attribute to a change in my feelings, but it

is not so.    What is good alone lives in my memory,
and not what is painful.    Pray impute therefore solely
to these hard times  my not more practically showing
my gratitude to you. on account of Carl.    God, however, directs all things, so my position may undergo
a favourable change, when I shall hasten to show you
how  truly  I am, with sincere esteem, your grateful
friend,

L. v. BEETHOVEN.

I beg you will read this letter to Carl.

### 209.

### *To G. del Rio.*

Carl must be at H. B.'s to-day before four o'clock; I
must request you therefore to ask his professor to dismiss
him at half-past three o'clock : if this cannot be managed
he must not go into school at all.    In the latter case I
will come myself and fetch him, in the former I will
meet him in the passage of the University.    To avoid
all confusion, I beg for an explicit answer as to what you
settle.    As you have been loudly accused of showing great
party feeling, I will take Carl myself.    If you do not
see me, attribute it to my distress of mind, for I am
now only beginning to feel the full force of this terrible
incident.*

In haste, your BEETHOVEN.

---

\* Probably the reversal of the first decree in the lawsuit with Carl's
mother, who in order to procure a verdict more favourable to her claims,
pointed out to the Austrian 'Landrecht,' where the lawsuit had been
hitherto carried on, an error in their proceedings, the 'Van,' prefixed to

210.

### To G. del Rio.

The assertions of this wicked woman have made such a painful impression on me, that I cannot possibly answer every point to-day; to-morrow you shall have a detailed account of it all; but on no pretext whatever allow her to have access to Carl, and adhere to your rule that she is only to see him once a month. As she has been once this month already, she cannot come again till the next.

In haste,

Your BEETHOVEN.

211.

### To Hofrath von Mosel.

1817.

Sir,

I sincerely rejoice that we take the same view as to the terms in use to denote the proper time in music which have descended to us from barbarous times.  For example, what can be more irrational than the general term *allegro*, which only means *lively*; and how far we often are from comprehending the real time, so that the piece itself *contradicts the designation*.  As for the four chief movements—which are, indeed, far from pos-

---

Beethoven's name, having been considered by them a sign of nobility. Beethoven was cited to appear, and on the appointed day, pointing to his head and his heart, he said, 'My nobility is here, and here.'  The proceedings were then transferred to the 'magistrate,' who was in universal bad odour from his mode of conducting his business.

sessing the truth or accuracy of the four cardinal points
—we readily agree *to dispense with them,* but it is
quite another matter as to the words that indicate the
character of the music; these we cannot consent to do
away with, for while the time is, as it were, part and
parcel of the piece, the *words denote the spirit in which
it is conceived.*

So far as I am myself concerned, I have long purposed
giving up those inconsistent terms *allegro, andante,
adagio,* and *presto;* and Maelzel's metronome fur-
nishes us with the best opportunity of doing so. I here
*pledge* myself *no longer* to make use of them in any of
my new compositions. It is another question whether
we can by this means attain the necessary universal
use of the metronome. I scarcely think we shall! I
make no doubt that we shall be loudly proclaimed as
*despots,* but if the cause itself were to derive benefit
from this, it would at least be better than to incur
the reproach of Feudalism! In our country, where
music has become a national requirement, and where
the use of the metronome must be enjoined on every
village schoolmaster, the best plan would be for Maelzel
to endeavour to sell a certain number of metronomes
by subscription, at the present higher prices, and as
soon as the number covers his expenses, he can sell the
metronomes demanded by the national requirements at
so cheap a rate, that we may certainly anticipate their
*universal use* and *circulation.* Of course some persons

must take the lead in giving an impetus to the undertaking. You may safely rely on my doing what is in
my power, and I shall be glad to hear what post you
mean to assign to me in the affair.

I am, Sir, with esteem, your obedient

LUDWIG VAN BEETHOVEN.

### 212.

*To S. A. Steiner, Music Publisher,— Vienna.*

Highest born! most admirable! and marvellous
Lieutenant-General! *

We beg you to give us bank-notes for twenty-four
gold ducats at yesterday's rate of exchange, and to send
them to us this evening or to-morrow, in order that we
may forthwith *remit* and *transmit* them. I should be
glad and happy if your trustworthy Adjutant were to
bring me these, as I have something particular to say
to him. He must forget all his resentment, like a good
Christian: we acknowledge his merits and do not contest his demerits. In short, and once for all, we wish
to see him. This evening would suit us best.

We have the honour to remain, most astounding
Lieutenant-General! your devoted

*Generalissimus.*

---

* Beethoven styled himself ' Generalissimus,' Herr A. Steiner ' Lieutenant-General,' and his partner, Tobias Haslinger, ' Adjutant' and
' Adjutant-General.'

### 213.

*To Lieutenant-General von Steiner.—Private.*

*Publicandum.*

After due consideration, and by the advice of our Council, we have determined and decreed that henceforth on all our works published with German titles, the word *Pianoforte* is to be replaced by that of *Hammer Clavier,* and our worthy Lieutenant-General, his Adjutant, and all whom it may concern, are charged with the execution of this order.

Instead of Pianoforte—*Hammer Clavier.*

Such is our will and pleasure.

Given on the 23rd of January, 1817, by the *Generalissimus.*

*Manu propria.*

### 214.

*To Steiner.*

The following dedication occurred to me of my new Sonata.

'Sonata for the Pianoforte,

or

*Hammer Clavier.*

Composed and dedicated to Frau Baronin Dorothea Ertmann—née Graumann,

by

Ludwig van Beethoven.'

If the title is already engraved, I have the two following proposals to make ; viz., that I pay for one title—
I mean that it should be at my expense, or reserved for
another new Sonata of mine, for which purpose the mines
of the Lieutenant-General (or *pleno titulo* Lieutenant-
General and First-Counsellor of State) must be opened to
usher it into the light of day. The title to be previously
shown to a good linguist. *Hammer Clavier* is certainly
German, and so is the device. Honour to whom
honour is due! How is it, then, that I have as yet
received no reports of the carrying out of my orders,
which, however, have no doubt been attended to ?

Ever and always your attached

*Amicus*

*ad Amicum*

*de Amico.*

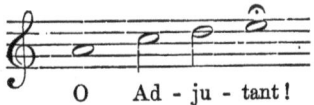

O    Ad - ju - tant!

N.B.—I beg you will observe the most profound silence
about the dedication, as I wish it to be a surprise !

215.

*To Zmeskall.*

Jan. 30, 1817.

Dear Z.,

You seem to place me on a level with Schuppanzigh, &c., and have distorted the plain and simple

meaning of my words. You are not my debtor, but I am yours, and now you make me so more than ever. I cannot express to you the pain your gift has caused me, and I must candidly say that I cannot give you one friendly glance *in return*. Although you confine yourself to the practice of music, still you have often recourse to the power of imagination, and it seems to me that this not unfrequently leads to uncalled-for caprice on your part; at least, so it appeared to me from your letter after my dedication. Loving as my sentiments are towards you, and much as I prize all your goodness, still I feel provoked!—much provoked!—terribly provoked!

Your debtor afresh,

Who will, however, contrive to have his revenge,

L. VAN BEETHOVEN.

END OF THE FIRST VOLUME.

LONDON
PRINTED BY SPOTTISWOODE AND CO.
NEW-STREET SQUARE

For EU product safety concerns, contact us at Calle de José Abascal, 56–1°, 28003 Madrid, Spain or eugpsr@cambridge.org.

www.ingramcontent.com/pod-product-compliance
Ingram Content Group UK Ltd.
Pitfield, Milton Keynes, MK11 3LW, UK
UKHW040616240426
470322UK00010B/161